MAX notes®

Virginia Woolf's

To the Lighthouse

Text by
Carolyn Coudert
(Ph.D., NYU)
Department of English
Project Blend-Bronx Borough High School
Bronx, New York

Illustrations by
Thomas E. Cantillon

Research & Education Association

MAXnotes® for
TO THE LIGHTHOUSE

Printed in the United States of America

Library of Congress Catalog Card Number 96-67414

International Standard Book Number 0-87891-054-9

MAXnotes® is a registered trademark of
Research & Education Association, Piscataway, New Jersey 08854

What MAXnotes® Will Do for You

This book is intended to help you absorb the essential contents and features of Virginia Woolf's *To the Lighthouse* and to help you gain a thorough understanding of the work. The book has been designed to do this more quickly and effectively than any other study guide.

For best results, this **MAXnotes** book should be used as a companion to the actual work, not instead of it. The interaction between the two will greatly benefit you.

To help you in your studies, this book presents the most up-to-date interpretations of every section of the actual work, followed by questions and fully explained answers that will enable you to analyze the material critically. The questions also will help you to test your understanding of the work and will prepare you for discussions and exams.

Meaningful illustrations are included to further enhance your understanding and enjoyment of the literary work. The illustrations are designed to place you into the mood and spirit of the work's settings.

The **MAXnotes** also include summaries, character lists, explanations of plot, and section-by-section analyses. A biography of the author and discussion of the work's historical context will help you put this literary piece into the proper perspective of what is taking place.

The use of this study guide will save you the hours of preparation time that would ordinarily be required to arrive at a complete grasp of this work of literature. You will be well prepared for classroom discussions, homework, and exams. The guidelines that are included for writing papers and reports on various topics will prepare you for any added work which may be assigned.

The **MAXnotes** will take your grades "to the max."

Dr. Max Fogiel
Program Director

Contents

**Each Chapter includes List of Characters,
Summary, Analysis, Study Questions and
Answers, and Suggested Essay Topics.**

SECTION ONE

Introduction

The Life and Work of Virginia Woolf

Adeline Virginia Woolf was born on January 25, 1882 in Kensington, London, the third child of Leslie Stephen and Julia Duckworth. One of the most prominent literary figures of the twentieth century, she is best known for her literary experimentation with a "stream of consciousness" form of writing. Her novel *To the Lighthouse*, published in 1927, is generally regarded as her most accomplished work. In addition to fiction, Woolf is admired for her literary criticism, essays and reviews, as well as her detailed literary journals, diaries, and letters.

Virginia Woolf's father, knighted in 1902, was an eminent man of letters, responsible for *The Dictionary of National Biography*. Her mother epitomized the Victorian ideal of femininity. (Mr. and Mrs. Ramsay, the main characters in *To the Lighthouse*, were based on her parents). The death of her mother when Virginia was thirteen followed by that of her beloved half-sister Stella, precipitated a breakdown which was the beginning of Woolf's life-long battle with depression and mental illness. Despite periods of illness, Woolf read voraciously, taking advantage of her father's extensive library. She was also tutored in Latin and Greek.

When Sir Leslie Stephen died in 1904, Woolf moved to Bloomsbury, London, with her half-brother, George, and his family. It was there that her brother Thoby's Cambridge friends began a series of "Thursday Evenings"—intellectual discussions in which Virginia was actively engaged and which formed the beginnings of the so-called Bloomsbury Group, known for its modernist, anti-Victorian approach to life and art. At that time also, Woolf began volunteer teaching at a college for working men and women. In 1910, Woolf became involved in the movement for women's suffrage. In the same year the First Post-Impressionist Exhibition received great attention and had a significant impact on the intellectual circles to which Woolf belonged. In later lectures and in her writing, Woolf commented that "human character changed on or about December, 1910." In 1912, Virginia Stephen married Leonard Woolf, an ex-colonial administrator, writer, and political thinker. *The Voyage Out,* her first novel, was accepted for publication.

Woolf's most serious mental breakdown, occurred in 1915, one year after Britain's entry into World War I. Following her recovery, the Woolfs' launched the Hogarth Press, publishing Virginia Woolf's first piece of experimental fiction, *The Mark on the Wall.* Her early novels, *The Voyage Out* (1915) and *Night and Day* (1919), were traditional in form. In *Monday or Tuesday* (1921), Woolf began experimenting with an expressionistic style, deliberately breaking from the Edwardian fiction of the time, as represented in the work of John Galsworthy (*The Forsythe Saga*). Woolf's objective is best summarized in her essay *Modern Fiction* (1919):

> For us at this moment the form of fiction most in vogue more often misses than secures the thing we seek. Whether we call it life or spirit, truth or reality, this, the essential thing, has moved off, or on, and refuses to be contained in such ill-fitting vestments as we provide.

In the novels that followed—*Jacob's Room* (1922), *Mrs. Dalloway* (1925), *To the Lighthouse* (1927), *The Waves* (1931), *The Years* (1937), *Between the Acts* (1941)—Woolf actualized her aesthetic inclinations. Not interested in plot, or other conventional elements which "embalmed" the whole, Virginia Woolf sought to convey, not contain, life. Her goal was not, as Woolf put it, to lead the reader to "write a check." (Writers like Arnold Bennett, H.G. Wells, and John Galsworthy who preceded Woolf, focused their attention on the material world and wished to move their readers to action.)

The term "stream of consciousness," which is frequently applied to Woolf's style, was coined by Willian James in his *Principles of Psychology* (1890) to describe "ceaseless, chaotic, multi-levelled flow that characterizes human mental activity." In the essay mentioned above, Woolf asserted that she was striving to record the atoms as they fall upon the mind in a way that revealed more than simply a personal vision. Woolf admired the work of James Joyce (*Ulysses*), T. S. Eliot (*The Waste Land*), and Joseph Conrad (*Heart of Darkness*), literary modernists who experimented with shifting time, multiple narrative voices, and complex allusions.

In addition to novels and short stories, Woolf published "The Common Reader" (1925 and 1932), and the now widely-read lecture *A Room of One's Own*, describing the challenges confronting women writers.

The catastrophe of the war years, beginning with Hitler's invasion of Austria in 1938, led the writer to sense an impending mental breakdown once again. In 1941, fearful of a recurrence of the mental illness which had plagued her for so many years, Virginia Woolf wrote a loving note to her husband, put heavy stones in her pockets and, walking into the River Ouse, drowned herself.

Historical Background

In order to fully understand the novel *To the Lighthouse*, three historical elements must be considered. The first element is Virginia Woolf's particular personal history. The second is the intellectual landscape directly preceding the novel's publication. And, thirdly, though in a certain respect, much less importantly, the world events which shaped the period.

Beginning with this last element, it has been said that Woolf didn't pay enough attention to the cataclysmic events happening in the world, specifically events preceding and following the first World War and preceding the second World War. The middle section of *To the Lighthouse, Time Passes*, contains a veiled reference to the first World War: "there came late in the summer ominous sounds like the measured blows of hammars on felt, which loosened the shawl and cracked tea cups." And then later we are told, in parenthesis, that Andrew Ramsay has been killed by a shell in France. The one allusion and the other matter-of-fact report are the only specific references to the war. Yet, the whole of *Time Passes* suggests, through atmosphere and imagery, the despair, the devastation, and the catastrophic consequences of the war. To judge the writer by the absence of literal references to war, is to miss her art entirely. Her indirect description of the climate of war, suggested by the empty house, ravaged by unseen forces, is a powerful metaphor of the death and destruction of war itself.

As noted in the preceding section, in a lecture to Cambridge undergraduates, Woolf commented, "On or about December, 1910, human character changed." A sense of precipitous change dominated the age in which Virginia Woolf lived and wrote. War increased the speed of industrial and social change. The writings of Karl Marx and Sigmund Freud opened up new ways of viewing human nature. In art, a move away from the representational and toward the communicative power of form over content occurred. The sense of a predictable world, anchored in tradition, disappeared.

Virginia Woolf was born when Queen Victoria was on the throne. By the end of her life, Woolf saw electricity replace gaslight, automobiles make the horse and carriage obsolete, and every aspect of social and cultural fashion alter. The end of the nineteenth century brought a break with the Victorian tradition of restraint and conventionality. In art as in life, previously held assumptions, approaches, and attitudes were questioned. Disillusionment with the limits of science, the newest god, as well as awareness of the need for social reform, were additional aspects of the times. This rebellion against Victorianism produced a confusing variety of literary forms, methods, and movements.

The dominant literary approaches during this time (1880-1914) were realism and naturalism. John Galsworthy (1867-1933) perfected the naturalistic novel, presenting characters in minute detail (an approach Woolf thoroughly repudiated). In addition, literary experiments with impressionism and symbolism were also popular. Following 1914, British literature became even more experimental and unconventional.

Although the historical context in which Woolf wrote was one of dramatic world events, Woolf's personal history and particular sensibility were probably the most important aspect of her writing. In *Moments of Being*, written in her fifties, she acknowledged her deep feelings about the "complete model of Victorian society" she experienced growing up. Yet, she understood that she was by nature one of her generation's "explorers, revolutionists, reformers". Her father, the quintessential Victorian male, aroused both admiration and rebellion in Virginia. She portrays that ambivalence in her protrayal of James and Cam in *To the Lighthouse*. When her mother died, her father's autocratic tendencies became more oppressive. Life at home was described by she and her sister, Vanessa, as unbearable. And, though she adored her mother, it was only through the writing of *To the Lighthouse* that she exorcised her mother's ghost. She understood that writing the novel provided an essential catharsis, as she used her parents as a prism to come to terms with her own conflicts about traditional male and female roles, to select what out of her early experience living in a Victorian world was worth keeping and what must be discarded, and to find her voice as an artist—as Lily Briscoe finally does in her painting.

Master List of Characters

Mrs. Ramsay—*Main character of the novel; 50-years-old; central force; nurtures family and house guests; demonstrates a heightened sensibility to nature and the needs of others.*

Mr. Ramsay—*Intellectual, viewed by children and others as somewhat harsh; unfeeling, fearful that he is unable to go much further with his scholarly endeavors.*

James Ramsay—*Six-year-old son of the Ramsays, youngest of eight; the most gifted of Ramsay children.*

Cam Ramsay—*Lively, devilish daughter of the Ramsays.*

Prue Ramsay—*Older daughter, with the beginnings of real beauty; dies in childbirth.*

Nancy Ramsay—*The Ramsays' daughter; avoids people and society by reading; confused by others' demands.*

Jasper Ramsay—*Shares his mother's love of exaggeration.*

Andrew Ramsay—*The Ramsays' son, killed in the war.*

Mary Ramsay—*The Ramsays' daughter.*

Rose Ramsay—*The Ramsays' daughter; attached to her mother; feminine.*

Charles Tansley—*Impoverished scholar; awkward, ridiculed by children; taken under Mrs.Ramsays' wing.*

Augustus Carmichael—*Philosopher; overweight; seems to be in drug-induced haze.*

Lily Briscoe—*Would-be artist, friend and admirer of the Ramsays', somewhat unattractive, resists cultivating feminine wiles, her search for an artistic vision is an important underlying theme.*

William Bankes—*Elderly widower, botanist, meticulous, lives in same rooming house as Lily Briscoe, met Mr. Ramsay many years before the present scene.*

Minta Doyle—*Young woman("tomboyish"); guest of the Ramsays; in Mrs. Ramsay's special protection; marries Paul Rayley.*

Paul Rayley—*Earnest young man, somewhat timid; courts Minta Doyle with Mrs. Ramsay's encouragement.*

Mrs. McNab—*The Ramsays' housekeeper; elderly woman who suffers aches and pains of age.*

Mrs. Bast—*Caretaker who assists Mrs. McNab.*

George—*Mrs. Bast's son.*

Mrs. Beckworth—*Houseguest; a kind, older woman who sketches.*

Mr. Macalister—*Seventy-five-year old fisherman; accompanies Mr. Ramsay and children to the Lighthouse.*

Macalister's son—*fisherman who accompanies the Ramsays on the boat.*

Summary of the Novel

To the Lighthouse is divided into three sections. The first section, *The Window*, takes up over half the book. In this section, we are introduced to all of the characters and become caught up in the web of relationships at the Ramsay's summer home. We see a day unfold with the promise of a trip to the Lighthouse (which never takes place), creating an underlying tension during the day. As the day unfolds, we see each of the characters from multiple perspectives. Each character's private mentations are recorded, as well as other characters' responses and interpretations of his/her behavior.

In this first section, Mr. and Mrs. Ramsay's relationship is highlighted, as well as their distinct personalities, i.e., Mr. Ramsay's idiosyncracies and Mrs. Ramsay's struggle to create harmony. Other characters are seen largely in their relationship to the Ramsays. We are watching the figures in this drama as if through a window. We get "inside their heads" as we hear their thoughts just as they occur to them.

The day passes. Mr. Ramsay takes his walks and ponders how he can push beyond "Q". Mrs. Ramsay flutters about her guests, meeting their needs. She reads a story to her son. The children romp and act mischievously. Romance is in the air as Mrs. Ramsay encourages Minta Doyle and Paul Rayley and Lily Briscoe and William Bankes. Dinner becomes an occasion; the *Bœuf en Daube* is prepared perfectly and spirits are high, rounded out with poetry, "And all the lives we ever lived and all the lives to be are full of trees and changing leaves." The children are put to bed. Mr. and Mrs. Ramsay sit, reading, he re-discovering Sir Walter Scott, she finding the "odds and ends of the day stuck to this magnet" a sonnet. The strength of their feelings for each other, bruised and scattered by the day, returns. There is a sense of contentment.

In the second section, *Time Passes*, Woolf takes an entirely different approach. In this section, an omniscient narrator dramatizes the decay of the house over a period of years. We learn that Mrs. Ramsay has passed away, Andrew has been killed in the war, and Prue has died in childbirth. The abandoned house is ghostlike: Nature predominates in this section. The house is now peopled by the dark, the rain, and the wind. Mrs. McNab, the housekeeper, is the only character who we experience in this section. She is the weathervane. She reminisces about Mrs. Ramsay and the mood of the house in former days.

> We *watch*—outsiders now- as time moves, with slowness immeasurable or with the speed of light, and the identities of the characters prevail only within parentheses.

The Lighthouse, the final section, takes place ten years after the beginning of the book. In this section, Lily Briscoe, is the central presence. It is through her struggle to create meaning of all this, the house, the family, her confused perceptions, that the novel comes to closure. Lily has her vision and completes her picture at the end. Mr. Ramsay is still brusque and demanding, but he finally manages to accompany James and Cam to the Lighthouse, even complimenting James on his sailing. James feels satisfied that he has reached the lighthouse: "It confirmed some obscure feeling of his about his own character." The journey, representing perhaps life's journey, has been long and fraught with difficulties, yet ultimately satisfying.

Estimated Reading Time

To the Lighthouse is divided into three sections. The first section is more than half the length of the book (143 pages). The second, and shortest section, is about 18 pages long. The third section is about 50 pages long. Each section is divided into relatively short sub-sections, 2-15 pages in length.

In order to fully appreciate the writer's style, *To the Lighthouse* needs to be read more slowly than books in which the plot is of central interest. Thus, although one could conceivably complete the book in six to seven hour-long sessions (reading approximately 30 pages an hour), a more leisurely reading pace would improve understanding.

If time is an issue, then it is suggested that the reader divide the first section approximately in half, planning then on four reading sessions of about an hour.

SECTION TWO

The Window

Chapters I–II

New Characters:

Mrs. Ramsay: *main character, mother of eight children*

James: *six-year-old son of the Ramsays*

Mr. Ramsay: *husband of the main character; a professor*

Charles Tansley: *student and protégé of Mr. Ramsay*

Augustus Carmichael: *philosopher-poet; house guest of the Ramsays*

Summary

Mrs. Ramsay sits with her six-year-old son James, who is cutting pictures from an army and navy stores catalogue. They are in the drawing room (living room) of their summer residence, a large, somewhat dilapidated house next to the sea on an island in the Hebrides (off the coast of Scotland).

The novel opens with Mrs. Ramsay's promise that they will sail to the Lighthouse the next day, if the weather is fine. Immediately after this exciting promise, Mr. Ramsay announces from just outside their window that "it won't be fine." James is crushed.

Charles Tansley, who is accompanying Mr. Ramsay on one of his frequent "walks", chimes in with his opinion that the wind is in the west, the worst possible direction for landing at the Lighthouse. Though exasperated with Tansley, Mrs. Ramsay reflects upon the

incivility of her children's mockery of the "uptight" scholar. She muses that she has the whole of the other sex under her protection as she admires their accomplishments, and she values their chivalrous attentions to her. Recognizing Tansley's awkwardness, she impulsively asks if he would like to accompany her on an errand. As the two set off, she asks Mr. Carmichael, who is seated on the lawn, if he needs anything in town.

Mrs. Ramsay shares with Tansley the belief that Carmichael should have been a great philosopher if it were not for an "unfortunate marriage." Charles begins to feel important because of Mrs. Ramsay's confidential manner. He experiences a strange excitement and imagines himself capable of great things, "even a professorship."

As the two walk on, they see an advertisement for a circus. Mrs. Ramsay exclaims delightedly that they all should go. As she senses his discomfort, she asks him to speak of his background and she realizes that ordinary childhood pleasures were not part of his early life. Her sympathies are further aroused.

When they reach the quay, Mrs. Ramsay exclaims about the beauty of the sand dunes and the bay. They observe an artist in a Panama hat and yellow boots, absorbed in his painting. She reflects that, since a well known artist had painted the area three years before, everyone was using the green and greys and soft lemons. Charles, now caught up in Mrs. Ramsay's magnetism, tries to see what she sees. He senses the contrast of his intellectual preoccupations with her aesthetic sensibilities and acute perception.

Tansley waits for his hostess as she visits a sick woman in the village. He absorbs the atmosphere of the poor woman's house and is attentive to Mrs. Ramsay's ministrations. He is overcome by her presence and her beauty, though "she was fifty at least" and had eight children. As they walk home, he experiences for the first time in his life an "extraordinary pride" in walking with a beautiful woman.

Analysis

The opening paragraphs of *To the Lighthouse* immediately establish the tension and the thematic elements of the novel. Mrs. Ramsay's lilting response to her six-year-old's wish to visit the

Lighthouse ("Yes, of course, if it's fine tomorrow," said Mrs. Ramsay. "But you'll have to be up with the lark," she added) is quickly superseded by her husband's intrusive reaction ("But, it won't be fine.").

The tension of this exchange foreshadows the novel's preoccupation with uncertainties, the future, how "things will turn out." The Lighthouse, in the midst of a perpetually changing sea, is a solid, if elusive, goal. The contrast in the parents' response to their son (she, enthusiastic and sensitive; he, careful and scientific) is a larger tension which operates throughout the book as a motif. (Which perspective, the personal or the scientific, represents "truth" or meaning?)

James, in the space of two minutes, undergoes feelings of sublime joy and feelings of overwhelming rage, to the point of imagining killing his father with an ax or a poker. Woolf's unique contribution is to lay bare the emotional intensity of the inner life of her characters:

> ...he belonged, even at the age of six, to that great clan which cannot keep this feeling separate from that...
> to such people even in earliest childhood any turn in the wheel of sensation has the power to crystallize and transfix the moment upon which its gloom or radiance rests... .

Woolf is able to crystallize these moments in her writing and illuminate the "wheel of sensation" as her characters move through their lives. For her, the plot does not center on action, but what happens inside her characters' heads.

The writer's ability to convey the essence of personality becomes apparent as we meet the secondary characters. Charles Tansley's "bony fingers," his physical "humps and hollows", his "parched, stiff words," as well as his "fidgeting, feeling himself out of things" create more than a visual picture: his view of himself and the world become physically palpable. Augustus Carmichael with "yellow cat's eyes ajar...(to give) no inkling of any inner thoughts or emotion whatsoever" and "sunk...in a grey-green somnolence which embraced them all, without need of words, in a vast and benevolent lethargy of well-wishing" is not only seen, but felt. Critics remark on Woolf's power to create these intense, "sensate" images.

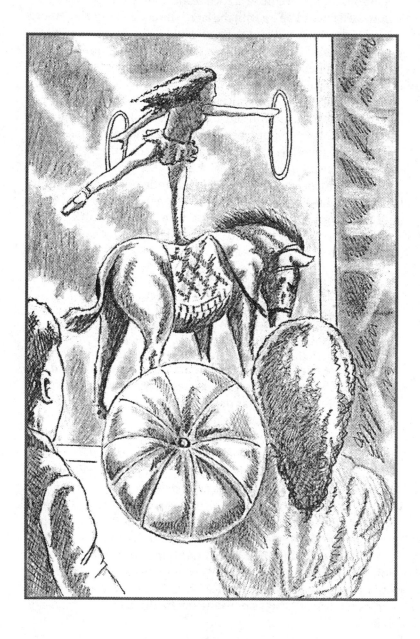

Mrs. Ramsay becomes a vehicle for Woolf to develop her literary perspective. Her perceptive and largely benevolent musings about the other characters, parallels Woolf's view of the world: the whole is more than the sum of its parts. Mrs. Ramsay (and Woolf) see the world as a kaleidoscope, constantly presenting alternative suggestions. Mr. Ramsay, on the other hand, prefers to make definitive judgments: "facts" were "uncompromising."

During the trip to the fishing village, Woolf further explores Mrs. Ramsay's highly tuned sensitivities and great personal magnetism. She (holds) "her black parasol very erect and (moves) with an indescribable air of expectation, as if she were going to meet someone round the corner." Mrs. Ramsay soothes Tansley's wounded ego and empathizes with a one-armed worker. She enthuses over the expectation of a circus; she changes continually her judgments of Tansley. She rhapsodizes over the beauty of the scenery and the color choices of an artist. She cheerfully ministers to a sick woman; and she engages the admiring glances of a ditchdigger. Woolf engages the reader through her minute-to-minute representations of Mrs. Ramsay's thoughts and feelings, until an intimate portrait emerges of an extraordinary woman.

The immediacy and intensity of Mrs. Ramsay's experience of the world echoes Woolf's writing style. Her goal is not to tell us everything about her characters or everything about what happens to them, but to re-create the fabric of their experience through, as she says "a myriad of impressions." The impact of her writing is closer to the intensity of poetry, than that of traditional narration. Musings are associational, not sequential, following the character's non-linear thought mechanisms. This "expressionist" form of writing may have been influenced by the work of William James, a distinguished psychological theorist who described the rapid movement of the mind as the "stream of consciousness."

Thus, this first chapter not only sets up the theme and tensions in the story, it introduces us to a very particular writing style. Mrs. Ramsay, the pivotal figure, personifies Woolf's novelistic style: keenly observant, reflective and sensitive, and capable of capturing the essence of a person or a natural setting in a highly evocative way. The underlying struggle between Mrs. Ramsay's highly intuitive responses and her husband's more carefully calculated,

logically "correct" observations foreshadow the psychological
struggle at the center of the novel: the strange admixture of emotional and intellectual and moral elements that undergird human
behavior.

Study Questions

1. Where does the novel take place?
2. Why is six year-old James disappointed?
3. How do Mr. and Mrs. Ramsay differ in their treatment of James?
4. Why do the children mock Charles Tansley?
5. Why does Mrs. Ramsay suggest that Tansley accompany her to town?
6. What explanation does Mrs. Ramsay give for Mr. Carmichael's lack of success?
7. What makes Mrs. Ramsay so attractive and magnetic to Tansley?
8. What entertainment does Mrs. Ramsay suggest to Mr. Tansley?
9. How does Woolf contrast Mrs. Ramsay's outlook with that of her husband?
10. How is Woolf's writing style different from more conventional writers?

Answers

1. The novel takes place at a beach house in the Hebrides (off the coast of Scotland).
2. James is disappointed because he wanted to sail to the Lighthouse the next day, but his father ruins his expectations, saying the weather won't permit it.
3. Mrs. Ramsay treats James with encouragement, recognizing his sensitivity. Mr. Ramsay ignores James' feelings, believing that facts are inviolate.

4. The children mock Tansley because he is serious and sarcastic. He can't play cricket and looks and walks funny.

5. Mrs. Ramsay invites Tansley to accompany her because she is aware of his discomfort and wants to include him.

6. Mrs. Ramsay tells Tansley that Mr. Carmichael is not a success, because he had an "unfortunate marriage."

7. Mrs. Ramsay is attractive and magnetic to Tansley because he feels flattered by her attention and infers through her conversation that she admires the masculine intellect. He is overcome with her beauty and feels important just walking beside her.

8. The entertainment that Mrs. Ramsay proposes is to go to the circus.

9. Woolf contrasts Mrs Ramsay's outlook with her husband's in the sense that she is more aware of people's feelings, more personally involved in encouraging and assisting others, and more attuned to the landscape. Mr. Ramsay focuses on abstract intellectual questions; he is preoccupied with his ability to contribute to the academic world.

10. Woolf's writing style is "stream of consciousness," rather than logically sequential in terms of plot or character development. She reveals her characters through recording the disconnectedness of their thoughts.

Suggested Essay Topics

1. Discuss how Mrs. Ramsay is viewed by her son, James; by Mr. Tansley; and by Mr. Carmichael. What is her own self-perception? As the reader, how do you see Mrs. Ramsay?

2. Provide at least three examples of Virginia Woolf's "stream of consciousness" writing. Explain how disconnected thoughts can reveal a character's personality.

Chapters III–IV

New Characters:

Lily Briscoe: *33-year old spinster; would-be artist, friend of the Ramsays*

William Bankes: *widower, old friend of Mr. Ramsay; botanist; lives in the same rooming house as Lily Briscoe*

Cam Ramsay: *the Ramsays' young daughter; lively and stubborn*

Jasper Ramsay: *the Ramsays' impetuous son*

Summary

Mrs. Ramsay, still sitting with James at the window, becomes suddenly aware of the cessation of voices and sounds which have provided a background. She is momentarily struck by an "impulse of terror." She quickly realizes that her husband and Charles Tansley have stopped their conversation. The sounds of the waves, which often provide a consoling "cradle song," now seem ominous, even ghostly. They seem to be beating out the measure of life. As she hears her husband's rhythmical walking and his half singing, half croaking chants, she feels comfortable once again. She finds a picture of a pocket knife for James to cut out.

Mr. Ramsay, caught up in some private rumination, suddenly calls out, "Stormed at with shot and shell." She's relieved that only Lily Briscoe, working at her easel on the lawn, was within earshot. Lily, she muses, isn't very attractive and would probably never marry. She remembers Lily's painting, and bends her head as Lily has requested her to pose.

Lily, though alarmed by Mr. Ramsay's sudden appearance and preoccupied raving ("Boldly we rode and well") is relieved he doesn't look at her picture. However, when William Bankes comes to stand beside her she is not so uncomfortable. She shares with him an easy familiarity based on their being neighbors and their similar styles: he scrupulous and judicial, she orderly and circumspect.

Mr. Ramsay again appears, wildly gestures, saying "Some one had blundered." Bankes suggests a stroll. Lily understands that he,

like her, feels uncomfortable and wants to get away. Still, she finds it hard to take her eyes off her painting. She agonizes over the difficulty of holding on to her vision. Despite the current fashion to emulate one Mr. Paunceforte who sees only pale, elegant, semitransparent colors, she doesn't want to deny the bright colors she sees, as well as the shapes under the colors. Still, her insecurities get the better of her. She thinks of her real life and feels a sense of personal inadequacy and insignificance.

The two, accustomed to this stroll, share a kind of exuberant joy in the sights and sounds of the bay: the waves, a fountain of water, a sailboat. They seem to be attuned in their musings, but Lily gazes at the sand dunes and thinks of eternity, while Bankes is reminded of a long ago incident in which Mr. Ramsay, walking along a road, spies a hen with her chicks. Ramsay had pointed his stick and said, "Pretty- pretty," Bankes felt Ramsay's sensitivity was revealed in that moment. Yet, somehow, since then, their friendship had become less real.

As William Bankes muses, he wonders if he has become dried and shrunk. He can't help comparing himself, childless and widowed, with Ramsay who has eight children. He is intrigued by the domestic demands, and shifts between envy and commiseration.

Lily and Bankes talk about Mr. Ramsay. Lily, though impatient with Mr. Ramsay's ridiculous behavior, still bids Bankes to "think of his work!" The image she holds in mind, when she tries to imagine Ramsay's work is that of a large kitchen table. Andrew had once told her that his father wrote about "Subject and objects and the nature of reality". When she didn't understand, he told her to "think of a kitchen table when you're not there." Lily, the artist, cannot imagine how one could reduce the color and beauty of nature to such angular essences, but accepts the importance of this perspective. Bankes, pleased with Lily's admiration of his friend, nevertheless returns to a thought he's had often before: Ramsay's best work is behind him.

As William Bankes ponders, Lily suddenly has an intense perception of her companion. She sees him as finer than Mr. Ramsay, heroic in his lack of vanity. Yet, after this first rush of admiration, she remembers certain pettinesses: he objected to dogs on chairs,

he complains about salt in vegetables. Her mind races; she asks herself, how do we judge people?

Her thoughts explode with intensity as a shot goes off. Jasper has shot a flock of starlings. Mr. Ramsay appears, distracted, booming, "Some one had blundered!" Though he looks at them for a moment, he is clearly in his own world, in the throes of some "delicious emotion."

Analysis

In this section, we see more deeply into Mr. and Mrs. Ramsay. Mrs. Ramsay feels an impulse of terror when the soothing background sounds momentarily cease. She is so sensitively attuned to all the nuances of the rhythms of her world—the voices, the footfalls, the multitude of personal habits of her family ("the taking out of pipes and the putting in of pipes")— that her usual composure is disturbed when things don't "sound right." This closer look shows us her exquisite sensitivity to the vibrations of life, as well as her vulnerability when this familiar world seems threatened.

Mr. Ramsay's preoccupations and eccentricities become more apparent now. He is caught up in a near trance-like re-creation of some historical scenes, shouting out snatches of poetry and gesticulating wildly. Yet, we also catch a glimpse of his sensitivity— Mr. Bankes' recollection of his delight with the chicks and his need for praise.

As we see their vulnerabilities—her dependence on the soothing noises of family life, his intellectual preoccupations which mute the emotional sensitivity he possesses—we begin to understand their mutual need for one another.

Lily Briscoe, preoccupied with capturing the truth, further illuminates the Ramsays. She notes Mr. Ramsay's vanity and ridiculous postures, yet, feels compelled to admire his intellectual aims, his "fiery unworldliness" as well as his love for children and animals. She adores Mrs. Ramsay, to the point of wanting to throw herself at her feet and shouting out her love. Yet, there is the hint of something else. (Her criticism of Mrs. Ramsay unfolds more slowly.)

Lily's quest, her insecurities and her counter-cultural viewpoint are really Virginia Woolf's own. She is the outsider, struggling to

honestly depict what she sees, always overcome with self-doubt, yet convinced that her vision is true.

William Bankes shows us Ramsay from a fellow intellectual's perspective. What had he gained and what had he lost by giving up intellectual isolation and surrounding himself by "clucking domesticity"? By following Bankes' "stream of consciousness," we see the author's extraordinary ability to reveal the strange and powerful connections the mind makes. Thus, Bankes saw a sand dune, thought of a road, remembered the road with the chicks, and ends up describing Ramsay's current state as "clucking domesticity."

Study Questions

1. Why does Mrs. Ramsay feel an "impulse of terror"?

2. Why does Mrs. Ramsay feel Lily will probably never marry?

3. What does Lily think of Mr. Ramsay?

4. Why doesn't Lily want to paint like the popular Mr. Paunceforte?

5. How do Lily Briscoe and William Bankes relate to one another?

6. Describe the view that Lily and Bankes look upon?

7. What is Mr. Bankes' relationship with Mr. Ramsay?

8. How does Bankes' view Mr. Ramsay's family responsibilities?

9. How does Lily compare Mr. Bankes and Mr. Ramsay?

10. Explain how Lily understands Mr. Ramsay's work.

Answers

1. Mrs. Ramsay suddenly notices the absence of household sounds. The sounds of her husband and Mr. Tansley and the children's playing have stopped and the sound of the waves startle her. She is reminded of the ephemeral nature of life. The day is slipping by, as is life.

2. Lily's "little Chinese eyes and her puckered-up face" seemed, at this moment, unattractive. She doesn't take Lily or her painting very seriously.

3. Lily recognizes that Mr. Ramsay is ridiculous in all his strange posturing and shouting, but she also admires his intellectual honesty.

4. Lily is very aware of the vibrant colors of the world, the purples and greens and whites. She feels that Mr. Paunceforte's pale colors don't match the reality she sees.

5. Lily and Mr. Bankes feel comfortable with one another. They live in the same rooming house and run into each other frequently. They are both rather sensible people, who respect each other's "no nonsense" approach to life.

6. Bankes and Briscoe look out on the blue waters of the bay. They see the very blue waters, the blackness of the waves, a fountain of white water, spurting behind a rock, a sailboat, the foam from the waves on the shore, the sand dunes in the distance.

7. William Bankes has known Mr. Ramsay for many years. He goes to some effort to keep the friendship alive, yet he knows that for a long time, their meetings have merely been repetition.

8. Bankes has no idea how Ramsay can feed eight children on philosophy. He is overwhelmed by the rough and tumble of the children and tries to remember their names through a kind of historical mnemonic. Yet he feels envious, too. He wonders how it would feel to have the affection of the children. He worries that he is dried and shrunk.

9. Lily sways in her estimation of the two men. She greatly admires Bankes' humility and lack of vanity, yet she recognizes a certain spark in Ramsay, a uniqueness that excuses his excesses.

10. Lily relies on Andrew's explanation of the metaphysical nature of Ramsay's work. She conjures up a scrubbed kitchen table, "Think of a kitchen table, when you're not there." Andrew's image ("Subject and object and the nature of reality") is imagined by Lily as a heightened visual experience. She compares this image to her own interest in color and form.

Suggested Essay Topics

1. How do William Bankes and Lily see Mr. Ramsay? What do they see as his strengths and weaknesses? What images do they each hold in thinking about Ramsay?

2. Mrs. Ramsay is very sensitive to sound. Discuss how her awareness and interpretation of the sounds of the waves, of people talking, and of her husband's pacing, creates a rhythmn in the novel.

Chapters V–VIII

Summary

Mrs. Ramsay soothes James again. She asks him to stand so that she can measure the stocking she is knitting against his leg. It is for the Lighthouse keeper's little boy. He fidgets and as she reprimands him, she looks up and notices how shabby the furniture is. Her thoughts race from the frustrations of housekeeping to her own inadequacies. (She never reads.) Things got shabbier and shabbier every summer. She frets over the children's messes, yet reminds herself that their hobbies are reflections of their giftedness. She agonizes over doors being left open and windows shut. She remembers that Marie, the Swiss maid, does love the fresh air. She thinks of Marie's father who is dying of cancer. The hopelessness of it overcomes her.

Her hopelessness is converted to irritation as she speaks sharply to her son. Sadness envelopes her. Her sadness is unfathonable to others. What personal tragedy has she suffered? She never discloses her private feelings.

William Bankes recalls a telephone conversation in which he was overcome by her voice. Her unselfconscious beauty intrigues him. She isn't interested in admiration; it bores her. Her hasty donning of the odd hat only contributes to her unique style.

Mrs. Ramsay kisses James on the head, smoothing out her earlier irritation. She asks him to find another picture to cut out.

She becomes aware of Mr. Ramsay. She knows by the "familiar signs" that he is unreachable. He nearly collides into Lily and

William Bankes; he is re-living Tennyson's poem "The Charge of the Light Brigade." ("Someone had blundered....Stormed at by shot and shell...boldly we rode and well...")

Mr. Ramsay comes out of his trance and his wife feels relieved that domesticity has triumphed. He brushes James' leg, but James recoils. Mrs. Ramsay comments that she's trying to finish the stockings to send to the Lighthouse tomorrow. Her husband is infuriated. How can she fly in the face of facts? He stamps his foot and says, "Damn you."

She feels overwhelmed ("dazed and blinded, pelted as with hail"). How can people pursue truth at the expense of human feeling? However, she says nothing to him. Abashed, he stands in silence and then humbly offers to call the coastguards. Feelings of reverence for him well up in her. He feels ashamed of his wild gestures. His whole mood changes.

Mr. Ramsay, fortified by the picture of his wife and son, returns to his earlier intellectual preoccupations. His image of the process of thought is like that of the keyboard of a piano, or like the alphabet. He feels he has reached the letter Q. Few people in the whole of England reach Q. He struggles in vain to reach R, but something like a shutter, or the eyelid of a lizard, obscures it. It is his fear of failure.

In his despair, he imagines himself as the valiant leader of a doomed expedition. He asks himself who will condemn the brave soldier who has fought valiantly and who now requires sympathy, whiskey, and an audience for his story? He feels justified in his need to stop, to gaze at his wife and son, and to do homage to the beauty of the world.

James is swallowed up in hatred of his father. He hates his egotism, his dramatic posturing, his interruptions; most of all he hates the way he disturbs his relationship with his mother. As her husband stops in front of her, James feels her tension. Yet, she pulls herself up and energy and life animate her. Mr. Ramsay wants sympathy. He tells her he is a failure. She exudes optimism and confidence in their life and he, reassured, is restored.

As he leaves to watch the children playing cricket, she is overcome with exhaustion. As she continues to read to her son, the waves sound ominous. She can't bear to feel finer than her husband, or, that others might believe he was dependent on her. She felt the burden of not being able to tell him the truth—that the greenhouse needed repair, that his last book was not his best. Feeling this burden, she gives in to some demon in her and calls out gratuitously to Mr. Carmichael, "Going indoors?"

She falls into a contemplation about Mr. Carmichael. Does the yellow stain on his beard mean he takes opium as the children believe? She knew he was unhappy. She senses he doesn't trust her. She blames this on the rejection and degradation he suffered under his overbearing wife. As she ponders in this way, she thinks that she never has trouble making people like her. She admits to herself that though her beauty can be a burden, it is nevertheless apparent. She is loved. She feels hurt that Mr. Carmichael shrinks from her. However, does this indicate her vanity? Did this show how flawed all human relations were, how shabby, how self-seeking?

Mr. Ramsay stops again, but does not speak. His plans are punctuated by the familiar path, the hedge, the urns. He ponders the significance of great men. He realizes that his thoughts will end up in his lectures in a month. He imagines himself on a horse, ambling through familiar lanes, in which are embedded historical poems and anecdotes. When he reaches the edge of the lawn and looks at the sea he drops the fantastical stories and posturing. He stands like a desolate sea-bird and the truth, that we know nothing and the sea, eats away the ground we stand on, is revealed to him. It is his ability to face the dark of human ignorance without compromise that inspires devotion in others. They are grateful that he serves as a kind of channel marker. Then, he turns and looks, once again, to his wife. He knows that he's unable—or unwilling—to forever contemplate these highly dignified themes. He finds consolation in family life, yet cannot own his own feeling, cannot say this is what I like.

Lily, putting away her things, reflects that the posture of the teacher or preacher transcends normal human ability. Perhaps reflecting on Mr. Ramsay's unusual behavior, she says to herself, "If you are exalted, you must somehow become a cropper."

Analysis

Family tensions are more fully revealed in these chapters. We feel the rage James feels toward his father and the deep division of sensibility in husband and wife. We also see Mr. and Mrs. Ramsay's deepest worries and fears. Woolf's highly developed "stream of consciousness" technique peels away layers of thought and feeling.

Mr. Ramsay, as seen by James, is a monster. His intensity disturbs the peace and rhythm he and his mother share. Woolf conveys James' acute sensitivity; he feels the nuances of his mother's posture as she responds to his father. The child's anxiety is conveyed by his body language: "By looking fixedly at the page, he hoped to make him move on; by pointing his finger at a word, he hoped to recall his mother's attention."

Mrs. Ramsay worries constantly. She worries about the house, the bills, her husband, her children's future, her own motives, the remorselessness of disease and death. She is often overcome with exhaustion from her efforts to soothe, to right things, to make people comfortable and happy. Most threatening of all to her is the worry that others feel that her husband is dependent on her. Woolf depicts Mrs. Ramsay as representative of the best of the Victorian woman; this role reversal is unthinkable to her. She needs to feel his superiority.

Mr. Ramsay, too, is preoccupied with worry. Is he a failure? The writer shows us his agitation through his habitual pacing and his fantasies. He throws himself into heroic roles in which he triumphs over great adversities. His wild "gesticulations" and his awkward physical intrusions, paint graphically the self-centered Victorian aristocrat. Though he views the mundane activities around him with the intellectual's disdain, he also senses that it is there that he finds beauty and comfort.

Woolf acknowledged that her portrait of Mr. and Mrs. Ramsay was based on her own parents. Her father, an intellectual, was seen as brusque and demanding by his children. Her mother was admired for her beauty, her social graces, and the depth of her commitment to the sick and needy.

The tension between Mr. and Mrs. Ramsay surfaces when she mentions casually that she's knitting the stocking to take to the

Lighthouse. He is enraged. He has already established that it will be impossible to make the journey; the weather is not favorable. His explosive, "Damn, you," reveals the depth of his anger at her dismissal of the facts. She, on the other hand, is equally enraged at his insensitivity. How can the facts be more important than people's needs or feelings? It is, however, in the rapidity with which the two completely reverse themselves, that Woolf reveals the strength of their bond. Though they can't budge on their principles, they move immediately on their deeper emotions. He feels terrible and offers to call the coastguard. She instantly feels only adoration.

Study Questions

1. Who is Mrs. Ramsay knitting for?
2. How does Mrs. Ramsay feel about the sea-side house?
3. Why does she speak sharply to her son?
4. How does Mr. Bankes feel about Mrs. Ramsay?
5. How does James feel about his parents?
6. Why does Mr. Ramsay say "Damn you" to Mrs. Ramsay?
7. What are Mr. Ramsay's thoughts as he paces through the garden?
8. How does Mr. Carmichael feel about Mrs. Ramsay?
9. Why is Mrs. Ramsay hurt by Mr. Carmichael's reaction to her?
10. What are Mr. Ramsay's thoughts at the end of this section?

Answers

1. Mrs. Ramsay is knitting a stocking for the Lighthouse keeper's son who has a tuberculous hip.
2. Mrs. Ramsay feels the house is shabby. She is frustrated by trying to keep the sea-dampness out of the house, by trying to get the family to cooperate to maintain the house.
3. She speaks sharply to James because she has been thinking about the death of Marie's father. She feels hopeless in the face of death.

4. Mr. Bankes is awed by Mrs. Ramsay's beauty. He compares her to a Greek goddess.

5. James feels rage towards his father and adoration of his mother.

6. Mr. Ramsay is frustrated by Mrs. Ramsay's unwillingness to accept the fact the weather will not permit a trip to the Lighthouse. He feels that she, and all women, tell lies.

7. Mr. Ramsay thinks about his intellectual ability and dramatizes passages from poetry.

8. Mr. Carmichael is indifferent to Mrs. Ramsay's ministrations. He is uncomfortable with her.

9. Mrs. Ramsay feels that people are attracted to her and she can't understand why Mr. Carmichael seems to reject her. It makes her wonder if he sees something that others overlook.

10. Mr. Ramsay looks at the sea and recognizes that, after all, human knowledge is very limited. It is his special gift to be able to see this so clearly.

Suggested Essay Topics

1. Despite her beauty and her roles as admired hostess and idealized mother, Mrs. Ramsay experiences frustration, sadness, and even pain. Trace the source of these feelings. What aspects of her personality contribute to these feelings? What elements of her domestic life further contribute to these feelings?

2. Mr. Ramsay also experiences deep frustration. What is the source of his frustration? How does he escape from his worries?

Chapters IX–XI

Summary

Mr. Bankes and Lily Briscoe discuss Mr. Ramsay. Bankes notes his peculiarities; Lily sees his narcissism as endearing, yet dislikes his narrowness. Bankes pushes Lily to see Ramsay as a hypocrite; Lily negates that idea. Then she thinks of the Ramsays "being in love" and is enraptured by the beauty of this idea.

Lily wants to critique Mrs. Ramsay, but refrains when she notices Bankes' "rapture." She appreciates his disinterested, "pure" pleasure in her beauty. However, as she turns to her painting, she is overcome with a sense of failure. She thinks again of Tansley's comment that women can't paint or write. Lily returns to her criticism of Mrs. Ramsay. Although she is very moved by Mrs. Ramsay's beauty, she thinks of her willfulness, her ability to ridicule, and her obsession with marrying everyone off, "presiding with immutable calm over destinies which she completely failed to understand." Still, Lily ponders the "essential spirit" of Mrs. Ramsay. She tries to fathom what it is about Mrs. Ramsay that seems to convey wisdom or knowledge. She remembers sitting at Mrs. Ramsay's knee, trying to capture her essence.

Mr. Bankes moves to look at Lily's picture. She flinches with the anxiety of revealing the "residue of her thirty-three years." Her friend is thoughtful and interested. He asks about the representation of Mrs. Ramsay and James as a triangular purple shape. Nervously, she explains that her purpose is not to depict them realistically, but rather to indicate their essence through line and shape and mass. She is profoundly grateful to share her most intimate vision with another human being. When Cam dashes past Lily, nearly knocking her easel over, Mrs. Ramsay reflects upon the distractedness of her daughter. Then her mind wanders to Minta Doyle and Paul Rayley who have gone off for a walk. She's anxious to know if Paul will propose.

James urges Mrs. Ramsay to continue with the story she is reading him. Mrs. Ramsay's thoughts, still on Minta and Paul, remembers her nickname for Minta's parents, the Owl and the Poker. She recalls private conversations with her husband in which she mimicked them. Her memory then skips to a comment by a woman who had accused her of "robbing her of her daughter's affection." Mrs. Ramsay becomes agitated as she recalls accusations that she is dominating and interfering. She thinks that she's only tyrannical about her social concerns, specifically hospitals and dairies. If she weren't so busy with her children, she would devote herself to reform in these areas.

Maternal devotion and joy is evident as she thinks of her childrens' talents and wishes that they'd never grow up. She is ready to dismiss the negative judgments as she revels in her children. Her joy in them is combined with a sadness, that they will never be so happy again. Mr. Ramsay becomes annoyed when she says that. She wonders if she isn't the more pessimistic of the two. Pondering about her combat with life, she admits that she sees life as terrible and hostile. Once again, Mrs. Ramsay becomes introspective. As she continues her reading to James, the light begins to fall and the darkness brings on a feeling of anxiety, which leads her to wonder again about Paul and Minta and Andrew.

When she finishes the story, James turns his interest to the lighting of the Lighthouse. She worries that he will ask again if they will make the trip the next day. She's relieved that the maid distracts him, but knows that he will remember that moment for the rest of his life. As she puts away James' pictures, she feels a sense of enormous relief to be alone. She is released from the strain of being and doing; she feels herself shrink to a "wedge-shaped core of darkness." Released from her attachments, her mind is free to roam. She experiences a feeling of infinite possibilities and a sense of stability. In this mood of reverie, she sees the third stroke of the Lighthouse which is her stroke. This long steady stroke somehow focuses her random thoughts into a phrase, "Children don't forget, children don't forget." Her internal dialogue continues and she says, "We are in the hands of the Lord."

Recoiling from this "insincerity," Mrs. Ramsay realizes that sometimes inanimate objects produced this intense sort of reaction. She asks, "How could any Lord have made this world?" She feels that there is no reason, or order, or justice; only suffering, death and the poor. As she thinks about this, her face becomes stiffened and severe. When Mr. Ramsay, lost in thought, passes by, he can't help but notice her sad expression.

Mrs. Ramsay moves out of these solemn thoughts when she notices the light again. Her identification, this time, takes a different form; she is overcome with the exquisite happiness she has known. As her thoughts turn to the joy she has experienced, Mr.

Ramsay notices her and marvels at her beauty. He chooses not to interrupt her daydreaming, but she, responding to his protectiveness, takes her shawl and joins him.

Analysis

In this section, we are given a more objective view of the Ramsays. Lily Briscoe, the artist, and William Bankes, the scientist, analyze their more subtle shortcomings and possible motives. Bankes, who has previously felt defensive about Mr. Ramsay, prods Lily to see him as a hypocrite. She, who has previously expressed only adoration for Mrs. Ramsay, wants to point out her obtrusiveness and her inclination to mock others weaknesses.

It is important to note Lily's authentic strength here. She puts aside her reservations, as she sees Bankes' "rapture" with the essence of Mrs. Ramsay. A true artist, she is able to put personal feelings aside, when in the presence of this kind of transcendent emotion. She is tuned into the power of truth and beauty, for "nothing so solaced her, eased her of the perplexity of life as this sublime gift." Lily's sensibilities and reverence for discovering the essence of life mirrors Woolf's life as a writer. Lily's struggle with her painting is becoming a central motif. She wants to paint as she, alone, sees (as Woolf wants to write as she sees). She wants to convey the essence of things, not merely the surface details. She works with color and shape and mass, impressionistically. We should note at this point that Woolf is using a similar technique with words. For example, we are shown, again and again, Mrs. Ramsay sitting at the window with James. We aren't given multitudinous details, but as we return repeatedly, we experience the mother and child as a kind of abstract presence.

Mrs. Ramsay's self-doubts and pessimism become more pronounced at this point. She resents the fact that others find her too strong-willed. She feels misunderstood. The depth of her pessimism becomes evident, too. She sees, most particularly, death, suffering, and poverty. She imagines suffering and loneliness for her children. The small space she has provided for James quickly evaporates as he sees the Lighthouse being lit. She understands how this disappointment will become symbolic: for the rest of his life, he'll remember this. Presumably, all his joy will be tinged by this moment.

Mrs. Ramsay's interior life is more fully revealed. Her craving for solitude and silence, as well as her ability to feel a kind of transcendence as she meditates on the Lighthouse, gives testimony to her depth. Despite what others may judge from her behavior, her depth and seriousness are revealed in her solitary reflections. The fact that she sees herself as a "wedge-shaped core of darkness," which echoes Lily's preoccupation with forms, suggests that she too has an aesthetic sensibility.

As Woolf delves further into Mrs. Ramsay's essence, the reader needs to reflect on Woolf's own personal and private persona. In letters and biographies, we learn that Woolf resorted to a social side which was a kind of camouflage for her intense interior life. She could be superficial and satirical with friends and take on a kind of social pose which might belie her real life which was exactly the opposite.

Study Questions

1. What is Lily Briscoe's criticism of Mrs. Ramsay?

2. What is William Bankes' criticism of Mr. Ramsay?

3. How does Mr. Bankes view Lily's work?

4. Why does Mrs. Ramsay feel misunderstood?

5. How does Mrs. Ramsay view life?

6. What does Mrs. Ramsay believe about James' disappointment with the postponed trip?

7. Why does Mrs. Ramsay like to be alone?

8. What does the Lighthouse represent to Mrs. Ramsay?

9. How does Mr. Ramsay feel about his wife's preoccupations?

10. Why does Mrs. Ramsay join her husband for a walk?

Answers

1. Lily feels Mrs. Ramsay is willful, capable of ridicule, and too preoccupied with arranging other people's lives (i.e., marrying them off).

2. William Bankes feels Mr. Ramsay is a hypocrite.

3. Bankes is interested in learning about Lily's painting. He listens to her ideas thoughtfully.

4. Mrs. Ramsay feels misunderstood by those people who accuse her of being domineering. She feels that she's only tyrannical about her social causes, for example, her hospital work.

5. Mrs. Ramsay feels life is terrible and hostile. She feels that there is no reason, or order, or justice—only suffering, death, and poverty.

6. Mrs. Ramsay believes that James will remember this day for the rest of his life.

7. Mrs. Ramsay likes to be alone because she feels released from the strain of being and doing. She experiences a sense of infinite possibilities.

8. Mrs. Ramsay endows the Lighthouse with a variety of symbolic attributes. The third stroke of the Lighthouse is "her stroke." In one instance it focuses her random thoughts into a phrase, "Children don't forget, children don't forget." At another moment, the light reminds her of the happiness she has known.

9. Mr. Ramsay notices his wife's preoccupations and is disturbed by her sadness.

10. Mrs. Ramsay senses her husband's protectiveness as he has glanced at her, marveling at her beauty. She takes her shawl and joins him.

Suggested Essay Topics

1. Based on what we learn about Mrs. Ramsay in these chapters, do you think she is misunderstood? Is she overbearing, even manipulative? How would you describe her motives?

2. Is Mrs. Ramsay more pessimistic than her husband, as she privately wonders? What evidence can you draw on to support or refute this judgment?

Chapters XII–XIII

Summary

Mrs. Ramsay takes her husband's arm and they go for an evening stroll. She speaks of her concerns about the gardener, but avoids once again speaking to him about the 50 pounds needed to fix the greenhouse. The two continue to chat about the children and the houseguests. As they talk, Mrs. Ramsay returns many times to her thoughts about the maintenance of the garden. As Mrs. Ramsay talks about the gardener, Mr. Ramsay chides her for exaggerating. When she protests, he takes advantage of the turn in the conversation to comment on her beauty. She turns the conversation to their daughter's beauty. Mr. Ramsay expresses his concern over Andrew's academic motivation. She defends him. Although they disagree, they are secretly pleased with the other's position. She worries about the group who have been gone for the afternoon. He begins to speak to her, but hesitates; she encourages him, and he tells her that he doesn't like to see her look so sad. They both become uncomfortable and drop the conversation.

Mrs. Ramsay wishes she had not been so unguarded. Mr. Ramsay decides that if she won't talk, then he'll return to telling himself the story of Hume being stuck in a bog. He thinks to himself that it's nonsense to be worried about Andrew and reminisces that at Andrew's age he was wandering the country all day with nothing but a biscuit in his pocket. This memory leads him to think about the freedom he enjoyed before marriage. He could "worry things out alone." This thought is quickly squashed, as he chastises himself for regretting his children.

Mrs. Ramsay guesses his thoughts and he objects that he knows he has nothing to complain of. He quickly kisses her hand intently. As they continue their walk, she reflects upon his youthfulness, though he is sixty. She reflects upon his detachment from ordinary things (he never notices anything), yet he shows keen insight into the extraordinary. She also worries that his habit of talking aloud or saying poetry was growing on him.

Mrs. Ramsay notices Lily Briscoe and Mr. Bankes and has a sudden vision that they will marry. Bankes talks to Lily about his travels as they stroll across the lawn. He suggests that seeing the Great Masters would be so important for her. Lily wonders if they wouldn't intimidate her. As the two turn and see the Ramsays, Lily has a sudden insight, "So that is marriage, a man and a woman looking at a girl throwing a ball." This scene captures the meaning, or symbolical nature of marriage for Lily. Though the moment is quickly broken, Lily holds on to this picture. She also predicts that Mrs. Ramsay has had the thought that she and Mr. Bankes will marry.

Analysis

Mr. and Mrs. Ramsay's marriage is seen more clearly. The bond they share is evident both in the spontaneous admiration they feel for one another and in the consideration they show one another. Though they have very different perspectives on life, they have chosen to repress their individual needs and responses in order to preserve their bond. They carefully skirt topics and issues they know are difficult for the other. Though their relationship is nurtured in this way, they maintain a certain distance from each other.

The Ramsays' marriage mirrors Woolfs' parents' marriage on many levels. Greatly infatuated with Julia Duckworth, Sir Leslie Stephen made a commitment to her that he would not ever interfere with her deeply felt avocation: her work with the poor and the sick. She, on the other hand, worried that she would not be able to be a proper wife to him as she felt deeply the loss of her first husband. Their sensitivity and respect for one another's needs was felt by all who knew them.

Lily Briscoe's sensibility parallels Woolf's own. The artist's ability to see in a momentary scene the encapsulation of a marriage echoes Woolf's desire to show the essence of a feeling or state through language.

Study Questions

1. What do Mr. and Mrs. Ramsay talk about during their evening stroll?

2. What worry preoccupies Mrs. Ramsay?

3. How do Mr. and Mrs. Ramsay feel about Prue? about Andrew? about Jasper?

4. What does Mr. Ramsay regret?

5. How does Mr. Ramsay feel about his family?

6. What are Mrs. Ramsay's feelings about her husband at this point?

7. What does Mrs. Ramsay hope about Lily and Bankes?

8. What scene captures Lily's attention?

9. What is this scene symbolical of for her?

10. What does Lily realize about Mrs. Ramsay's thoughts about her and William Bankes?

Answers

1. Mr. and Mrs. Ramsay talk about the garden, the children, and their houseguests.

2. Mrs. Ramsay is preoccupied with the 50 pound bill for the greenhouse. She is also concerned about all aspects of the upkeep of the garden.

3. Mrs. Ramsay worries about Jasper shooting birds. Mr. Ramsay believes it is just a stage. Mrs. Ramsay believes Prue is a great beauty; Mr. Ramsay hasn't noticed it. Mr. Ramsay worries about Andrew's efforts to obtain a scholarship; Mrs. Ramsay doesn't value this one way or the other.

4. Mr. Ramsay laments the loss of his solitude, his ability to think his own thoughts without interruption.

5. Mr. Ramsay feels a deep devotion to his family and chastises himself for sometimes wishing they weren't there (so he could work, uninterrupted).

6. She admires his youthfulness. She marvels at his unusual mind, yet knows that he's totally unaware of the world around him. She's concerned about his talking to himself.

7. Mrs. Ramsay has a sudden insight that Lily and Bankes will marry.

8. Lily is struck by the scene of Mr. and Mrs. Ramsay watching their children playing catch.

9. Lily sees this scene as somehow representing what marriage is about: a man and a woman watching their children.

10. Lily suddenly realizes that Mrs. Ramsay will be thinking that she and Bankes should marry.

Suggested Essay Topics

1. What do you believe is the secret of the Ramsays' successful marriage? Describe how they interact with each other. Why are boundaries important in marriage? Was this a typical Victorian marriage?

2. When Lily observes Mr. and Mrs. Ramsay watching the children play catch, the scene takes on a symbolical meaning for her. Discuss why this particular scene might have appealed to her artistic sensibility.

Chapters XIV–XVI

New Characters:

Minta Doyle: *emotional young woman; impulsive, outspoken*

Paul Rayley: *earnest young man; timid*

Nancy Ramsay: *pensive; prefers solitude*

Andrew Ramsay: *interest in collecting marine life; somewhat aloof*

Summary

All of Chapter XIV is written within parentheses. Minta, Paul, Andrew, and Nancy take an afternoon's excursion. Minta coerced

Nancy into joining them. Nancy would have preferred retreating to the attic. She feels pressured by the demands of socializing.

Andrew observes that Minta is a good walker, dressed in a short skirt and black knickerbockers. He likes her rashness, but believes it will get her into trouble. Andrew notes that Minta doesn't seem to mind what she says or does. Minta pitches down on the edge of a cliff and starts singing, "Damn your eyes, damn your eyes." Andrew wants to reach the good hunting grounds, before the tide comes in. Paul reads from a guidebook about the islands being celebrated for their marine curiosities. They all slide down the cliff. On the beach, they separate. Andrew takes his shoes and socks off and goes to the Pope's Nose. Nancy wades out to some rocks and pools. She broods over the pools, listening to the waves, and is struck by the vastness of the world and the tininess of the pool. Andrew shouts that the sea is coming up. He and Nancy, running to the shore, come upon Minta and Paul in each other's arms. Brother and sister are deeply embarassed.

When they reach the top of the cliff, Minta cries out that she's lost her grandmother's brooch. She weeps dramatically and they all go back and look for the brooch. As the tide comes in, Minta suddenly shrieks in terror, "We shall be cut off!". Andrew is annoyed that she has no control of her emotions. Paul reassures her that he will get up at daybreak and search for the brooch.

They walk up the hill. When the lights of the town come out beneath them, Paul sees the lights as all the things in the future that will happen to him: his marriage, his children, his house. He feels overwhelmed by the day. He is anxious to tell Mrs. Ramsay that he has asked Minta to marry him. As he sees the house all lit up, he is giddy with excitement. However, he subdues these feelings, not wanting to make a fool of himself.

Mrs. Ramsay, sitting at her dressing table, worries again about the excursion. Could they have drowned? She feels alone in the presence of her old, antagonist life. Jasper and Rose come into her room, wanting to know if Mildred should hold dinner. "Not for the Queen of England," she responds, aware of her tendency to exaggerate. She has Rose pick out which jewels she should wear to dinner. Worrying about the dinner, she reflects that the *Bœuf en Daube* is Mildred's masterpiece and must be served on time. As Mrs.

Ramsay considers Jasper's choice of the opal necklace and Rose's choice of the gold, she glances out of the window and sees with amusement the rooks trying to decide which branch to settle on. She calls the father rook, old Joseph, and the mother Mary. She loves the movement of the wings, beating out.

The mother urges the children to choose her jewels. She lets Rose clasp her choice against her black dress. She thinks how important this ritual is for Rose. How at this point in her life, the child feels such a deep feeling for her mother. Mrs. Ramsay feels sad, that it was so out of proportion to anything she was. She asks Jasper to take her arm, and Rose to carry her handkerchief. She thinks, as she asks Rose to choose her a shawl, that Rose, being female, will suffer so. They stop by the window on the landing and look at Joseph. Mrs. Ramsay asks Jasper if he doesn't think the birds suffer, having their wings broken. He thinks that birds don't feel, but he likes her stories of Joseph and Mary.

Mrs. Ramsay hears the travelers. She is annoyed with them now, but descends the stairs like a queen who accepts the tribute of her people gathered in the hall. She notices the smell of burning and worries about the dinner. The dinner gong calls everyone in the house to let go of their private activities and assemble for dinner.

Analysis

In the excursion to the beach, we see the children and Minta and Paul away from the confines of the house. We feel the presence of the ocean, the cliffs, the climbing rocks, and the small pools. We also see both the influence of the parents on the children and their uniqueness. Andrew's reaction to Minta, and to all women, is much like his father's. Nancy, though more naturally reclusive than her mother, shares her mother's ability to project onto nature moods, feelings, and meanings.

Mrs. Ramsay's strong influence is felt as Paul's insecurities about "taking the plunge" surface. If it weren't for her, he might never have had the courage to propose. The maternal insight of Mrs. Ramsay is nowhere clearer than when she encourages Rose to choose her jewels. Without any narcissism, she knows that at this stage, her daughter's feelings for her are very deep. She allows room for that and only feels saddened by the discrepancy between what Rose feels and how life will treat her. Mrs. Ramsay's sense of humor, rarely seen, is suggested by her fantasy about Joseph and Mary.

Study Questions

1. Why didn't Nancy want to go on the walk?
2. What is Andrew interested in on the walk?
3. What is Paul's purpose in this excursion?
4. What personality characteristics does Minta exhibit?
5. What does Minta lose on the beach?
6. What does Paul promise to do?
7. Rose and Jasper help Mrs. Ramsay to choose what?
8. Why does Mrs. Ramsay allow Rose to select her jewels?
9. What creatures does Mrs. Ramsay talk to?
10. In what way does Mrs. Ramsay walk down the stairs?

Answers

1. Nancy finds Minta too demanding. Nancy prefers to be alone.
2. He is interested in collecting marine specimens.
3. Paul wants to ask Minta to marry him.
4. Minta is emotional, somewhat rash, and a bit pushy.
5. Minta loses her grandmother's brooch.
6. Paul promises to return at daybreak to find the brooch.
7. They help her choose a necklace.
8. Mrs. Ramsay knows this ritual is important to her. She is in a stage of "mother worship."
9. Mrs. Ramsay talks to the rooks who settle on the trees outside the window.

10. Mrs. Ramsay walks down the stairs like a queen who silently accepts her subjects' adoration.

Suggested Essay Topics

1. Chapter XIV takes place away from the house and Mrs. Ramsay's presence. Andrew and Nancy are more individuated, as are Paul and Minta. Nevertheless, Mrs. Ramsay's influence is still felt. In what way are the events of the day and the reactions of the participants influenced by Mrs. Ramsay?

2. Mrs. Ramsay is particularly responsive to Jasper and Rose when they join her in her dressing room before dinner. What is the significance of this scene? Why do you think Woolf has chosen to provide us with this particular glimpse of Mrs. Ramsay?

Chapter XVII

Summary

Mrs. Ramsay takes her place at the head of the table. She thinks to herself, "But, what have I done with my life?" Mr. Ramsay, at the far end of the table, is slouched down and frowning. She can't remember why she ever felt any emotion for him. As family and guests come into the dining room, one after the other, she thinks, "It's all come to an end." As she ladles the soup, she thinks there is no beauty anywhere. She feels exhausted, just trying to keep things going.

Lily Briscoe notices how old and worn and remote Mrs. Ramsay looks. When Mrs. Ramsay speaks to William Bankes, Lily senses that she pities him and feels it is a typical misjudgment of Mrs. Ramsay's. Lily respects the fact that he has his work, which makes him not pitiable at all. She thinks of her own work and sees that it, too, is a treasure. She muses about her painting and has an insight about placing the tree more in the middle of the picture.

Charles Tansley fumes silently; he thinks the dinner table talk is just rot. He is annoyed by the women who he thinks make

civilization impossible with all their "charm" and silliness. Lily, looking at Tansley's hands and nose, thinks him the most uncharming
of men. His comment that women can't write or paint, still rankles,
but she determines to put it aside and think of her painting: that
matters, nothing else. Tansley, feeling her insincerity as she offers
to accompany him to the Lighthouse, is annoyed. He wishes he
were alone, working.

Bankes and Mrs. Ramsay talk about Carrie Manning who has
written to William Bankes. Mrs. Ramsay hasn't seen her in 20 years
and is intrigued by the gossip William shares: the Mannings are
building a billiard room, and they are very well off now. Mrs.
Ramsay can't believe the Mannings have had lives that she hasn't
known about. Bankes is uncomfortable with all the waiting and
talking. He wonders if family life is somehow trifling and boring
compared with work. It is an effort to make himself socialize. Mrs.
Ramsay uses her "social manner" to ask him if he detests dining
in the "bear garden." Bankes, becoming more uncomfortable,
politely denies this.

Unable to speak in these social codes, Tansley thinks what
nonsense is being talked. He fantasizes how he will report this
evening to his friends. He will say how Ramsay had "dished" himself by marrying a beautiful woman and having eight children.
Still, he feels left out of the conversation about the fishing industry. Lily, sensing Tansley's discomfort, resists helping him out of
his discomfort. She thinks about the roles men and women play:
what if women didn't help men out of these social situations and
men didn't help women out of the Tube when it was on fire?

Mrs. Ramsay asks Tansley if he's planning to go to the Lighthouse and if he's a good sailor. Tansley, ready to explode, says he's
never been sick a day in his life. Lily, responding to Mrs. Ramsay's
desperate signals, relents and offers a kind word to Tansley, who
then joins in the conversation. He tells about visiting his uncle who
kept a lighthouse. Lily feels she has had to pay a price for being
nice: she has not been sincere. She thinks that most relationships
between men and women are insincere. She then, happily, turns
back to thoughts of her painting. Tansley continues talking, beginning to enjoy himself. Mrs. Ramsay goes back to her memories of
the Mannings' drawing room 20 years ago.

The talk at the table becomes centered on the declining fishing industry and then moves to politics. William Bankes, Lily, and Mrs. Ramsay feel bored, but Bankes, always fair-minded, tries to listen to Tansley. He thinks that perhaps the young man is knowledgeable and that despite his bad manners, may turn out to be a man of genius in the world of politics.

Mrs. Ramsay wishes that her husband would say something. She feels that what he says goes to the heart of things, that he really cares about the fishermen. As she thinks of her husband's intelligence and authenticity, she glows with admiration. However, at that moment, Mr. Ramsay is scowling and frowning. She realizes that he is furious that Augustus Carmichael has asked for another plate of soup. Ramsay can't bear waiting for people to eat when he has finished. He is about to explode, she senses, but he holds himself back. The couple, looking at each other down the length of the table, know exactly what each other is thinking. The children are close to bursting with laughter as they watch their father about to erupt. Mrs. Ramsay asks for the candles to be lit. She decides that she respects Augustus for being above public opinion; she admires his composure.

The bowl of fruit at the center of the table draws her attention. She and Augustus silently admire this yellow and purple dish of fruit in the candlelight. It looks like Neptune's banquet. The candlelight brings the faces closer round the table. The dark night is shut out and the group becomes conscious that they are a party. It is as if they are stranded on an island together. The maid carries in a large dish; Minta and Paul arrive and take seats at opposite ends of the table.

Minta laments her lost brooch. Mr. Ramsay teases her gently and she feels confident of her attractiveness. Mrs. Ramsay, seeing Minta's glow, feels jealous. She knows that her husband likes these golden-reddish girls who didn't "scrape their hair off." She feels a little resentful that she has grown old, but is grateful to these lively girls for bringing out the youthfulness in her husband. She remembers his gallantry when they were young. As the maid puts the *Bœuf en Daube* on the table, she motions to Paul to sit beside her. She thinks that she sometimes prefers her "boobies" to all these clever men with their dissertations.

Paul's reference to "we" is enough to tell Mrs. Ramsay that he's proposed. As she prepares to serve the meal, the moment becomes an occasion. She feels two emotions; one the profound sense of the joining of a man and a woman, and the other, a sense of a kind of mockery, as these two enter into an illusion.

Mr. Bankes declares the dish a triumph. His previous impatience with Mrs. Ramsay's social manner disappears, and his adoration returns. Mrs. Ramsay, buoyed up by William's renewed enthusiam and affection, begins to laugh and mock and gesticulate. Lily thinks there is something frightening about her; she puts a spell on them all. Yet, she contrasts Mrs. Ramsay with her own poverty of spirit and feels left out.

Lily's emotions become feverish. She thinks that when she's with the Ramsays she feels two things at the same time: "that's what you feel and that's what I feel." Lily thinks about love and marriage and wonders if women don't feel "this is not what we want." When the conversation turns to coffee and cream, and Mrs. Ramsay expresses her deep concerns about the iniquity of the English dairy system. The children and Mr. Ramsay laugh at her. Mrs. Ramsay notices Lily's distance from the group, but thinks that, despite Minta's glow this evening, Lily will be the better at forty. Mrs. Ramsay admires Lily, but decides most men won't see her unique charm, except perhaps Mr. Bankes. She decides that William must marry Lily. She must arrange a long walk for them soon.

Mrs. Ramsay begins to plan a picnic for the next day. She feels optimistic. Everything seems possible. Her thinking becomes almost euphoric: she feels secure, solemnly joyful, looking at all of them eating there. The moment brings a feeling of coherence and stability. It is this moment of peace, she decides, which allows that which endures. She is vaguely aware of the intellectual conversation at the table (square roots and Voltaire and Napoleon, and the French system of land tenure). She feels the support of this masculine intelligence.

William Bankes praises the Waverly novels. Tansley denounces them. Mrs. Ramsay knows that it is Tansley's insecurity which drives him so fiercely to assert himself. Someone asks how long Scott's novels will last. Mrs. Ramsay senses her husband will fasten onto this issue of literary longevity. Paul Rayley speaks with obvious feeling about books which impressed him as a boy. His honest response contrasts with Tansley's need to impress.

Mrs. Ramsay turns her gaze back to the fruit bowl. Rose has taken a pear. She is surprised that her own child has disturbed the composition. She looks at the children sitting silently in a row, with the hint of a joke between them. She thinks that Prue is envying Minta. She thinks, you will be happier than she is one day, because you are my daughter.

She is ready to get up, but the others are still involved in spirited conversation. She thinks that Mr. Ramsay is in great spirits this evening. She hears all the voices as voices at a cathedral. Then her husband recites some poetry and the line, "All the lives we ever lived and all the lives to be are full of trees and changing leaves." These words, like music, have been in her mind all evening.

Augustus gets up and chants the end of the poem, and bows to her and holds the door open. She pauses at the threshold, holding on to the scene which is vanishing. As she takes Minta's hand, she realizes, looking over her shoulder, that it is now in the past.

Analysis

The dining room scene is the culmination of the day. The group moves from irritation and detachment to connection and harmony. Private soliloquies of the day are abandoned, the meal and conversation is shared. Like survivors on an island, they sit together in the circle of light at the table. The evening becomes an occasion, an evening to remember.

Like survivors, they have moved through perilous waters. The island metaphor is rich in meaning. They are literally on an island; they have also created an island within the island which has provided a place to temporarily put to rest individual battles. The evening progresses from isolation and dissatisfaction to community and harmony.

Mrs. Ramsay's mood at the start of the meal is despondent. The worries and misunderstandings of the day have accumulated. She asks herself what she has done with her life and thinks, "it's all come to an end."

Lily is annoyed with Mrs. Ramsay's narrowmindedness. Tansley is disgusted with the small talk. Mrs. Ramsay is taken aback when she learns that Carrie Manning has a billiard room. Bankes is bored with the waiting and talking. Mr. Ramsay is enraged when Carmichael asks for a second plate of soup. Then the candles are lit. Mrs. Ramsay and Mr. Carmichael notice the eloquence of the bowl of fruit. Minta arrives and Mr. Ramsay's mood improves as he teases her. The *Bœuf en Daube* is pronounced a triumph. Mr. Bankes recovers his adoration of Mrs. Ramsay. Paul indicates that he has proposed. Mrs. Ramsay is buoyed up by the prospective marriage and Mr. Bankes' improved mood.

Woolf's dramatization of this evening suggests a well-constructed play. The players arrive from disparate places, disconnected and preoccupied with private griefs. As the meal progresses, they experience a growing sense of well being and rapport. We see that Mrs. Ramsay's ability to create this harmony is her special gift. Hearing their voices as voices in a cathedral, we feel her importance as a synthesizer, an artist of human relations. Her husband's poetry captures the essence of the evening and of the events of the day, "All the lives we ever lived and all the lives to be are full of trees and changing leaves." The setting and ambience of the scene are so vividly etched in our minds that at the end, when Mrs. Ramsay pauses at the threshold, wanting to hold on to the scene, it is as if a curtain has gone down for the reader, too.

Study Questions

1. What does Mrs. Ramsay feel at the beginning of the dinner?

2. What does Lily observe about Mrs. Ramsay?

3. What are the thoughts of Tansley? of Bankes?

4. What are Lily's thoughts about the relationships of men and women?

5. What is discussed at dinner?

6. What are Mrs. Ramsay's thoughts about her husband's silence?

7. What happens when the candles are lit?

8. What has happened to Paul and Minta during the afternoon?

9. What are Lily's thoughts?

10. What is Mrs. Ramsay's feeling about the evening?

Answers

1. Mrs. Ramsay feels exhausted and discouraged. She wonders what she's done with her life and doesn't feel any emotion for her husband.

2. Lily observes that Mrs. Ramsay looks tired. She senses that she pities Mr. Bankes.

3. Tansley can't stand the superficiality of the conversation; he thinks that women make civilization impossible. Bankes is bored and uncomfortable with all the talking.

4. Lily feels that relationships between men and women are basically insincere.

5. Talk at the dinner table is of politics and the declining fishing industry.

6. Mrs. Ramsay wishes her husband would talk, because she feels his words are sincere and pointed.

7. When the candles are lit, the faces around the table seem closer together. The dark night is shut out and the group becomes conscious of their relationship together.

8. Paul and Minta have become engaged.

9. Lily is disturbed by Mrs. Ramsay's power over the group. In contrast to her exuberance, Lily feels a poverty of spirit. Her emotions become feverish as she recognizes the conflict between her own wants and what the Ramsays seem to require.

10. Mrs. Ramsay feels optimistic and joyful, watching her guests eat. She feels that this moment of peace allows that which endures.

Suggested Essay Topics

1. In an essay, explain why the dinner scene is pivotal to the novel. Explore how it pulls together the loose ends of the day. What is Woolf saying about human needs?

2. Create a one-act play based on Woolf's description of this scene. If you are interested in film, identify the kinds of shots and transitional cuts necessary to convey Woolf's depiction of this scene.

Chapters XVIII–XIX

Summary

As the dinner scene fades, Lily watches Mrs. Ramsay ascend the stairs in the lamplight. She notices that her departure brings a kind of disintegration to the group; they scatter. Bankes takes Tansley by the arm and continues the dinner table conversation about politics. The shift from "poetry to politics" strikes Lily. She wonders where Mrs. Ramsay is going so quickly.

Mrs. Ramsay is reflective. She seeks to sift through the evening and pick out the "thing that mattered" from the evening. Her internal "judges" query her: Is it good? Is it bad? She uses the branches of the elm trees outside to anchor her. She approves of the dignity of the trees' stillness. It is windy, she notes. She concludes suddenly that for as long as they lived, they would remember this night, the moon, the wind, the house, and her. She feels a sense of community and happiness: all of this was theirs, and Paul and Minta would carry it on when she was dead.

Entering the nursery, Mrs. Ramsay is annoyed to find the children still awake at 11:00. They are arguing about the boar's skull, hanging on the wall. Cam is frightened by the shadows which fill the room; James screams if anyone dares to touch it. Mrs. Ramsay covers the skull with her shawl and soothes Cam by chanting a rhythmical story about fairies living in the "bird's nest" that the draped skull suggests. Cam falls asleep. James, reassured that the skull is still there, asks if they will go to the Lighthouse tomorrow. She admits that they won't go tomorrow, but on the next fine day. Again, she thinks that he will never forget this and is angry with her husband, Charles Tansley, and even herself for raising his hopes.

Mrs. Ramsay closes the nursery door and thinks about Charles Tansley in the room above. She hopes he won't bang his books and wake the children and once again lists for herself his faults and his virtues. She notices the yellow harvest moon through the staircase window. Prue, watching her mother from below, is overcome with love and admiration. Prue says that the group may go down to the beach to watch the waves. Mrs. Ramsay with a sense of revelry, urges them to go. When she asks if anyone has a watch, Paul Rayley pulls a gold watch out of his wash-leather case. Mrs. Ramsay feels Minta is lucky to be marrying a man with such a watch.

Mrs. Ramsay exclaims that she wishes she could go, but she feels held by something very strong. Still smiling, she goes into the room where her husband is reading. Entering the room, she has a vague feeling of wanting something. Mr. Ramsay, absorbed in his reading, clearly doesn't want to be interrupted. She sits down and takes up her knitting. Then she realizes that he is deeply into a Sir Walter Scott novel and is most probably trying to determine if Tansley was right: people don't read Scott anymore. She knows he is comparing his work to Scott's. She is troubled about her husband's preoccupation with measuring his worth: will he be read? are his books any good? why aren't they better?

Mrs. Ramsay thinks, "What does it all matter?" However, she is reminded of her thoughts at dinner, how she admires his unflinching truthfulness; she trusts him. She sinks deeper into a reverie, again wondering what it is she wants. Half sleeping, half knitting, the rhythmic lines of poetry seem to move from side to side in her mind. She reaches for a book, murmuring,

And all the lives we ever lived
And all the lives to be
Are full of trees and changing leaves,

As she reads at random, she feels as if she's moving from branch to branch of her mind, from one red flower to one white flower. Mr. Ramsay slaps his thighs and their eyes meet. They do not want to speak to each other just now, but something seems to go from him to her.

Mr. Ramsay, overcome with the strength and simplicity of Scott's writing, feels "roused and triumphant." He becomes choked

with tears, and hiding his face with his book, lets them fall. He
thinks that it doesn't matter a damn who reaches Z ("if thought
ran like an alphabet from A to Z"). Finishing the chapter, he feels
as if he's been arguing with someone and now has got the better of
him. Still, he decides he must read it again, keeping his judgment
in suspense. Determining not to bother his wife again with his
worries about young men not reading his books, he turns to look
at her. He thinks she looks peaceful and is glad that the others have
taken themselves off and that they are alone. He muses that the
whole of life doesn't consist of going to bed with a woman.

Mrs. Ramsay, still caught-up in a kind of dream state, feels as
if she's climbing the branches of a tree, laying hands on one flower,
then another. She comes upon a sonnet ("Nor praise the deep ver-
milion in the rose") and suddenly feels that the odds and ends of
the day are put in order by the sonnet form. It has captured the
essence of life and created a beautiful, rounded, clear, and complete shape. She becomes conscious of her husband looking at her;
smiling, he seems to be gently mocking her for falling asleep. Mr.
Ramsay, pleased to see that she doesn't look sad now, thinks that
she is astonishingly beautiful. At the same time he thinks that she
probably doesn't understand what she's reading: he likes to think
of her as not clever or book-learned.

Mrs. Ramsay puts the book aside and asks, "Well?" She takes
up her knitting again and tries to remember what has happened
since they've been alone together. Her mind lights on a list of random, unrelated events, i.e., dressing for dinner; the moon; Andrew
holding his plate too high at dinner; being depressed by something
William had said; the birds in the trees; the sofa on the landing;
the children being awake; Tansley waking them with his books falling on the floor. She wonders what she should tell him about. She
speaks of Paul and Minta, saying they are engaged. He says he's
guessed as much, but his mind is still with Scott, hers with the
poetry. Then she becomes aware that she wants him to say something, anything. She mentions Rayley's watch in the wash-leather
bag, trying to summon up the kind of joking they have together.
He only snorts; she wishes even more for him to say something.
He senses her imminent "pessimism" and fidgets. Finally he says
that she won't finish that stocking tonight. Mrs. Ramsay realizes

that that was what she wanted: the asperity in his voice, reproving her. She decides that if he says it's wrong to be pessimistic, then it is wrong; she decides the marriage will turn out all right. Mrs. Ramsay agrees that she won't be able to finish the knitting. She senses that his look has changed and that now he wants her to give him what she finds it difficult to give: to tell him that she loves him. She thinks that she can never say what she feels and that he has often reproached her for this, calling her heartless.

Mrs. Ramsay gets up and stands at the window, looking at the sea. She feels herself to be very beautiful, knowing that her husband is thinking that of her. Mr. Ramsay thinks, would she not once tell him that she loved him. She cannot say it. She turns and looks at him, beginning to smile, knowing that, though she has not said a word, he knows that she loves him. She looks out of the window again, thinking that nothing on earth can equal this happiness.

At this moment Mrs. Ramsay says, "Yes, you were right. It's going to be wet tomorrow. You won't be able to go." As she looks at him smiling, she feels she has once again triumphed: she has not said it: yet he knew.

Analysis

The concluding chapters of *The Window* bring closure. The dinner is over, the day is completed, and most importantly, both Mr. and Mrs. Ramsay bring their internal struggles to rest. They are able to turn to each other in love and admiration.

Lily Briscoe's perspective opens Chapter XIX. As Mrs. Ramsay ascends the stairs, Lily wonders why it is that Mrs. Ramsay inevitably moves with a kind of secret mission and that her sudden comings and goings change the balance of everything surrounding her. As she sees it, the dispersement of the group marks a change from poetry to politics. Lily is attuned to Mrs. Ramsay's role as a kind of plumb line, her aesthetic sensibility senses the shape and form of the interactions with Mrs. Ramsay.

Interestingly, contrary to Lily's assumption, Mrs. Ramsay's departure was motivated, not by an urgent errand, but by her need for an aesthetic pulling together of the bits and pieces of the day. The writer's interest in going beneath appearances is evident here. Even if Lily's intuitions about the shape of things—the underlying pattern—is largely correct, her interpretations of discrete moments doesn't necessarily have to be accurate. (Like the novelist, the artist may convey a truth, but not all the truth.) Once again, Mrs. Ramsay is drawn to the branches of the elm trees. She finds a kind of stability in the trees, but now instead of noticing the crows jumping from place to place, she finds her thoughts jumping from branch to branch. Woolf's ability to create this kind of internally generated metaphor, is an indication of her skill in using the "stream of consciousness" technique.

It should also be noted that Mrs. Ramsay, who represents the quintessential mother, often turns to nature or the physical world, to anchor her internal confusion. She finds meaning, or peace, or solace in the physical world: the ocean, the trees, the crows, the wind. Everything, in fact, that is concrete speaks to her: her mother's sofa, her father's rocking chair, Paul's wash-leather bag, and, of course, the Lighthouse.

The scene in the nursery is an intimate one. It is here (as it was when she allowed the children to choose her jewelry) that we see her entering into the imaginations of her children. She is a gifted mother, intuiting the needs of each child. She respects James' need to have the skull remain; she helps Cam move beyond her fright, not merely by comforting, but by engaging with her in an idyllic redirection of her imaginings. She empathizes, once again, with James: he will never forget this day, the day his hopes were dashed.

It's no wonder that, as she descends the stairs, noting the "yellow harvest moon" through the window on the landing, Prue thinks that there is only one person in the world like her mother. She becomes a child again, never wanting to give up this maternal comfort. Virginia Woolf's loss of her own mother, when she was a bit younger than Prue, is evoked here. The writer, as well as her sister, Vanessa, acknowledge that Mrs. Ramsay was a portrait of their beloved mother.

When Prue says that the group is thinking of going down to the beach to look at the waves, Mrs. Ramsay becomes "like a girl of twenty, full of gaiety." We are reminded of her enthusiasm about the circus in the first chapter. She is able to identify with both the joy and the pain of those she loves. We are also reminded of Woolf's description of James on the first page of the novel: "He

belonged to that great clan which cannot keep this feeling separate from that...any turn in the wheel of sensation has the power to crystallize and transfix the moment upon which its gloom or radiance rests." Like James, Mrs. Ramsay responds immediately to the moods and actions of those around her.

In the closing scene, the needs and deeper feelings of the couple are met. In their own private worlds, he reading Scott, she reading poetry, they work through their tangled feelings. Mr. Ramsay is re-fueled; the truth of Scott's work is there for him. He lets go, at least for today, the need for the world's praise and can finally turn to his wife with pleasure and appreciation. The sonnet she reads finally pulls together for her the rag-tag remnants of the day into a meaningful whole. She, like Lily, needs to organize all of the miscellany into a shape. Her confusing thoughts are swept clean. She can turn to her husband and smile and enjoy the warmth of his love.

The day has come full circle. The tensions felt on the first page of the novel are somehow resolved. He has been able to let go of his harsh self-judgment—the basis of his impatient reaction to the "irrationality" of his son and wife. He doesn't need to be told: he knows she loves him, and that's enough. She has been able to put to rest her incessant worrying, sensing that the harmony of the whole transcends the cacophony of the part. She responds now to her husband's greater self: his honesty and integrity.

Study Questions

1. What is on Mrs. Ramsay's mind as she ascends the stairs?

2. Why are the children still awake at 11 p.m.?

3. How does Mrs. Ramsay comfort Cam? James?

4. How does Mrs. Ramsay feel about her guests going to the beach at night?

5. What is Mr. Ramsay doing in the drawing room?

6. What occupies Mrs. Ramsay's mind, as she sits near her husband?

7. What is Mr. Ramsay's conclusion about Sir Walter Scott's novel?

8. What does Mrs. Ramsay read?

9. What impact does Mrs. Ramsay's reading have on her?

10. What enables Mr. and Mrs. Ramsay to feel re-united at the end of this section?

Answers

1. Mrs. Ramsay is trying to identify something meaningful out of the events of the day.

2. James and Cam are still awake because they are fighting about the boar's head skull on the wall. Cam is afraid of the shadows it makes on the wall; James refuses to have it removed.

3. Mrs. Ramsay places her shawl on the skull so that James' need is met: it is not removed. She makes up a fanciful story, filled with birds and trees and fairies, so that Cam sees the shape, not as menacing, but as beautiful.

4. Mrs. Ramsay is almost girlish in her enthusiasm. She becomes very animated as she encourages them to embark on this marvelous adventure.

5. Mr. Ramsay is deeply engrossed in reading one of Sir Walter Scott's novels.

6. Mrs. Ramsay feels distracted, trying to figure out what it is she wants.

7. Mr. Ramsay concludes that no matter what the current fashion is, Scott's simplicity and passion and ability to move are unparalleled.

8. Mrs. Ramsay picks up a poetry book to read.

9. After reading randomly a number of verses, a sonnet strikes her as conveying the essence of life. She feels satisfied and rested.

10. The fact that each has untangled some of his/her own thoughts and are able to appreciate their life, enables them to turn, once again, to each other.

Suggested Essay Topics

1. The scene in the nursery suggests the power of Mrs. Ramsay's maternal instincts. How does this scene, coupled with the scene in her dressing room prior to dinner, illuminate Mrs. Ramsay's extraordinary empathy? Do these scenes provide the reader with a more accurate picture of Mrs. Ramsay than her own ruminations?

2. The close of the day finds Mr. and Mrs. Ramsay in the library. How do each of them put to rest the turmoil of the day? What is a prerequisite to their drawing closer? What, do you surmise, is Woolf's definition of a happy marriage?

SECTION THREE

Time Passes

Chapters I–VII

New Character:

Mrs. McNab: *elderly caretaker; suffers aches and pains of age*

Summary

Some years after the day recorded in *The Window*, Andrew and Prue Ramsay, as well as Mr. Bankes, Mr. Carmichael and Lily Briscoe, return to the seaside house. Mr. Bankes remarks, as he enters the house, "Well, we must wait for the future to show." The others comment on the extreme darkness of the evening. When they're all safely indoors, they extinguish the lights and retire for the evening.

After this brief glimpse of the characters met in *The Window*, Nature becomes personified as the main character of *Time Passes*. The "immense darkness" and the wind invade and explore the house "ghostly, as if they had feather-light fingers and the persistency of feathers." They surround and touch the sleeping figures, the furniture, and all of the inanimate objects. These elements of nature sigh and murmur, asking, "How long would they endure?" The night is superseded by a restless passing of many nights. Autumn follows summer and the trees "take on the flash of tattered flags." Nights become filled with "wind and destruction." The sea tosses and frustrates any would-be seeker of truth.

We learn that Mrs. Ramsay has died rather suddenly one night, at an indeterminate point within this passage of time. (This, and

all other references to the fate of the family, is given in parentheses.) The "stray airs" continue to move ceaselessly through the
rooms. They explore the remnants of the former inhabitants, the
clothes they have shed and left. These are the only reminders of
life. Then, after the wind has examined all aspects of the deserted
house, loveliness and stillness take over and the restless questions
seem to fade.

Mrs. McNab, the caretaker, breaks the silence as she enters the
house to open the windows, and dust the bedrooms. She moves
awkwardly through the house, dusting and singing. She is toothless, witless, and bowed down with weariness. She lurches "like a
ship at sea" and leers " aimlessly smiling." Though her 70 years have
not been easy, she possesses a vague happiness.

Spring comes. (Prue Ramsay has married.) As the season ma-
tures, Nature is once again personified. With the awakening of the
earth, hopefulness, happiness, goodness, and order seem to return.
Yet, as spring departs, she averts her head and seems to take upon
herself the "sorrows of mankind." Summer follows spring and we
learn that Prue has died in childbirth. At night the Lighthouse
throws a stroke across the carpet and bed. Mrs. Ramsay's shawl,
hanging on a hook, loosens and sways in the wind. The long summer days bring the hum of flies and the yellow haze of the sun.
But, later in the summer, ominous sounds menace the summer
days. (Andrew Ramsay has been killed by a shell in France.)

The beauty and harmony of the sights and sounds of summer—the sea, the sunset, the fishing boats, the children on the
beach—is marred by the sounds of war. (Mr. Carmichael has published a volume of poetry.) The seasons repeat themselves, yet
"month and year ran shapelessly together" as if the universe were
battling in brute confusion. The flowers and trees continue to
bloom, but it is as if they exist in emptiness. Chaos seems to rule.

Analysis

Time Passes is a short poetic interlude which functions to make
important connections between the first and last sections of *To the
Lighthouse*. Using an omniscient narrator, Woolf dramatizes the
decay of the house, which is neglected for ten years. Left to the

forces of Nature, the abandoned house comes perilously close to absolute disintegration.

In *The Window*, all of the movement was forward: the anticipation of the trip to the Lighthouse, Mrs. Ramsay's fantasies for her children, the future estimation of Mr. Ramsay's work, Minta and Paul's engagement, and so on. In *Time Passes*, the movement of Time only serves to erode and destroy. The remnants of human habitation in the house suggest, not only decay, but death.

Virginia Woolf creates powerful visual images as she personifies the darkness enveloping the house and the sea air intruding into every empty inch. The havoc wrought by the elements of Nature is meant to parallel the events taking place in the larger world. The forces of destruction, so overpowering during these war years, come perilously close to threatening civilized life. It is a dark time, a dark night. As the wind moves through the house, toying with a flap of wallpaper and rustling papers in the wastebasket, it questions, "Were they allies? Were they enemies? How long would they endure?" Thus, Mr. Bankes' opening remark, "Well, we must wait for the future to show," and the falling of the immense dark in the house, suggest the uncertainties and fears experienced in the world at large.

There is another, more personal form of darkness, which is intimated here. *To the Lighthouse* is Woolf's re-creation of her early life and her reminiscences of her parents. *Time Passes* suggests Woolf's struggle with her personal darkness. She spoke often of the ghostly presence of her beloved mother, as well as her mourning for her brother, Thoby, and her half-sister, Stella.

Study Questions

1. What two aspects of Nature invade the house in Chapter II of *Time Passes*?

2. How are these aspects of Nature personified? What do they do?

3. In Chapter III, "divine goodness" is personified. What does it do?

4. What do the "stray airs" in Chapter IV find in the house?

5. Describe Mrs. McNab, the care-taker.

6. What do we learn about Prue Ramsay in Chapter VI? about Andrew Ramsay?

7. What change does summer bring in Chapter VI?

8. In a passage near the end of Chapter VI, we are told "the mirror has broken." What is the mirror? Why has it broken?

9. What explanation is given for the publication of Mr. Carmichael's poems.

10. In Chapter VII we learn that night and day, month and year run shapelessly together? What is the reason for that?

Answers

1. The aspects of Nature which invade the house are the dark and the wind.

2. The darkness creeps in the keyholes and crevices, steals round window blinds, swallows up jugs and basins and flowers, and furniture. The wind creeps around corners, ventures indoors, questions and wonders ("Would the wallpaper hang much longer?"), smoothly brushes the walls, asks the wallpaper and books and letters, "How long will they endure?"

3. Divine goodness parts a curtain, displays a wave falling, a boat rocking; he twitches the cord and draws the curtain. Our penitence and toil have awarded us only a glimpse.

4. The stray airs find hangings that flap, wood that creaks, bare legs of tables, saucepans and china, furred, tarnished, cracked. Only the clothing that people have left—shoes, a shooting cap, faded skirts and coats—retain a human shape.

5. Mrs. McNab is 70-years-old, toothless, bonneted, and bowed down with weariness. She lurches from side to side of the stairs; she leers at herself in mirrors.

6. Prue Ramsay has died in childbirth. Andrew Ramsay was killed by a shell in France.

7. Summer brought ominous sounds like the measured blows of hammers dulled on felt which seemed to have the effect of repeated shocks, so that the flapping shawl was further loosened, more tea cups were cracked.

8. The meaning which mankind finds in nature is like a mirror. When all human meaning has departed (the mindlessness of war), then mankind cannot find meaning in Nature.

9. The success of Mr. Carmichael's poems was attributed to the war; people said that war had revived people's interest in poetry.

10. The natural rhythms of the universe, day and night, seasonal change, are disturbed by the universe battling and tumbling in brute confusion and wanton lust, aimlessly.

Suggested Essay Topics

1. Discuss in detail how Nature is personified in *Time Passes*. Include in your discussion an analysis of why the writer might choose to use Nature as the main character in this section.

2. Compare and contrast the story development in *The Window*, with the story development in *Time Passes*. What is the difference in point of view? in thoughts about Nature? In thoughts about the future?

Chapters VIII–X

New Characters:

Mrs. Bast: *caretaker, born in Glasgow; did not know the Ramsays; assists Mrs. McNab*

George: *Mrs. Bast's son; quiet, hard worker*

Summary

Mrs. McNab has heard that the family will never come again. She picks some flowers to take home with her. She wonders what will happen to the house. She looks at the moldy books and knows they should be laid out on the grass in the sun. Talking to herself, she thinks that the war and the difficulty in finding help, have rendered the house beyond repair. It's beyond her strength to do it. But, why hasn't anyone come to see it? Why did they leave clothes in all the bedrooms? She thinks that poor Mrs. Ramsay won't want them again; she has been dead for years. Mrs. McNab fingers Mrs. Ramsay's grey gardening cloak. She remembers her in the garden as she walked up the drive with the washing. She knows that once they had planned to come to the house, but the war made travel impossible.

Mrs. McNab recalls the day that she brought the washing. Mrs. Ramsay had asked the cook to keep a plate of soup for her. She thinks how all the help liked Mrs. Ramsay, she had a pleasant way with her. As she thinks of Mrs. Ramsay, she thinks how much has changed. Prue and Andrew are dead, and there have been so many other losses during the war. Prices had gone up and never come down. She is despairing as she looks at the falling plaster, where the rain has come in. It was too much for one woman to repair. She locks the house and leaves.

The deserted house degenerates even further. It was left like a shell on a sandhill to fill with grains of salt now that life has left it. The night and the airs seem to have triumphed. What power could prevent the fertility, the insensibility of nature? Mrs. McNab's memories are not powerful enough to stay the rack and ruin. Only the Lighthouse beam enters the house for a moment, looking with calmness at the decay.

The fate of the house is poised, a feather could change the balance. A feather could result in the house pitching into darkness. Stray picnickers or lovers or tramps might take over. The roof might cave in, briars and hemlocks might cover the steps and windows. A broken china cup might be the only evidence of human habitation a trespasser might discover.

Suddenly, a letter from one of the young ladies requests that the house be put to order. Mrs. McNab and Mrs. Bast, old and stiff, with creaking legs, are set to work. They become the force that stays the rot; they rescue the house from the pool of Time. A kind of laborious birth takes place. Together with Mrs. Bast's son, George, they slowly return the house to life.

The two women pause sometimes for tea, contemplating their magnificent conquests and their partial triumphs. As they rescue the books from spiders and pale mushrooms, she remembers Mr.

Ramsay, lean as a rake, talking to himself on the lawn. He had never noticed her.

Mrs. McNab remembers the pleasant times in the house—the kind cook with the sense of humor who saved delicious morsels for the help. She thinks they lived well then. Mrs. Bast, who never knew them, asks about the beast's skull. Mrs. McNab tells her that the Ramsays had friends in eastern countries, perhaps one of them had brought it. She remembers the gay evenings with ladies in evening dress and jewelry. She would be asked to do the washing up and might stay as late as midnight. Mrs. Bast comments that they'd find it changed.

As she watches George scything the grass, she thinks again that they'd find it changed, referring to the grounds. Old Kennedy, who was supposed to have charge of it, had fallen from a cart and couldn't work.

At last, after days of labor, the task is finished. There seemed to arise a kind of melody, an intermittent music of barking, and humming and all manner of sounds which the ear strains to bring together in harmony. Then, as evening falls, quiet descends. (Late one evening in September, Lily Briscoe had her bag carried up to the house.)

Messages of peace breathe from the sea to the shore. As Lily lays her head on the pillow, she senses that the murmuring messages are the voices of the beauty of the world. The house is full again and the voices seem to be entreating the sleepers to go out and see the night, with head crowned and scepter jewels ready to meet the eyes of a child. If the sleepers didn't awaken, the voice, without complaint would continue to lull them. Gently the waves would break and tenderly the light would fall. Mr. Carmichael, shutting his book, thinks it looks much as it used to look.

Nothing disturbs the sleepers until the early morning arrival of the birds, the sun, a cart grinding, and a dog somewhere barking. Lily stirs, clutches her blankets, like a faller on the edge of a cliff, and then sits bold upright in bed, awake.

Analysis

Mrs. Mc Nab, picking flowers and laying them on the table, presides over a kind of funeral: the family will not return, never

again. She asks herself what she is to do with the abandoned clothing like a widow, wringing her hands at her husband's death. Woolf's repetition of words, "It was too much for one woman, too much, too much," creates a kind of lamentation. Woolf's elegy on the deserted house is nothing short of poetry:

The house was left; the house was deserted. It was left like a shell on a sandhill to fill with dry salt grains now that life had left it... The swallows nested in the drawing room; the floor was strewn with straw, the plaster fell in shovelfuls; rafters were laid bare; rats carried off this and that to gnaw behind wainscots. Tortoise-shell butterflies burst from the chrysalis and pattered their life out on the windowpane. Poppies sowed themselves among the dahlias; the lawn waved with long grass; giant artichokes towered among roses; a fringed carnation flowered among the cabbages; while the gentle tapping of a weed at the window had become, on winter's nights, a drumming from sturdy trees and thorned briars which made the whole room green in summer.

The omniscient narrator tells us that total dissolution of the house might be caused by as little as one feather, tipping this perilous scale. However, there was a "force" working. Suddenly one of the young ladies wrote to Mrs. McNab. "Would she see that the house was ready? Would she get this done; would she get that done; all in a hurry."

Ironically, it is Mrs. McNab and her co-worker, Mrs. Bast who become the force to save the house from total ruin. Their age and their physical condition make them unlikely heroines. They are not attractive figures: they creak, they leer, they hobble, they lurch; they are toothless and dimwitted. They do not go about their work "with dignified ritual or solemn chanting." Yet, like dumb forces of nature, they reverse the decay and save this microcosm of civilization.

When we contrast the attractiveness and intelligence of Mr. and Mrs. Ramsay in *The Window*, with the decrepit caretakers in *Time Passes*, we are stunned. Virginia Woolf's brilliant creation of the two haggard women is masterful. The personalities in *The Window* are vibrant and alive. Mrs. McNab and Mrs. Bast, in contrast, suggest nothing so much as old crones, rattling around a haunted house. All that is left of Mrs. Ramsay is her shawl, flapping on the door. Mr. Ramsay's precious books are covered with mold and spiders. These ghost-like reminders suggest that philosophy can't save us; the social fabric, elegantly embroidered though it may be, can't save us. However, sometimes, if we are lucky, forces far removed from our planning and understanding step in.

Despite their groaning and stumbling, the caretakers, like old soldiers, ("...breaking off at mid-day with the smudge on their faces, and their old hands, cramped with the broom handles. Flopped on chairs ...") are revived as they restore the house. They chat, they remember the good times, they feel triumph in their success. Life is resurrected through them. Woolf is saying, indirectly, yet profoundly: war is ugly, it results in havoc and destruction and the recovery from war is not pretty or dignified, but the life force, this time at least, prevailed.

We learn, as soon as the caretakers have finished, that peace has come. Lily Briscoe, returning to the house, sleeps wrapped in the gentle and kindly arms of the night. The arduous task of restoring the house, parallels the exhausting struggle of war. Things have, finally, been put right. Nature no longer bodes ill, but offers comfort and beauty. The long hard night is over. Morning breaks. The artist who seeks a vision wakes up. Life has returned.

Study Questions

1. What are Mrs. McNab's thoughts on returning to the house?

2. What are Mrs. McNab's memories of Mrs. Ramsay?

3. Explain the metaphor of the the feather. What does it signify?

4. Why do Mrs. McNab and Mrs. Bast and her son come to clean the house?

5. How does Mrs. McNab remember Mr. Ramsay?

6. How does Mrs. McNab remember the house when the Ramsays were there?

7. What personal handicaps do the two women have in their housecleaning efforts?

8. What is suggested by the words, "messages of peace breathe from the sea to the shore"?

9. How does nature change as a result of these messages?

10. Describe the sleep enjoyed by Lily when she returns to the house.

Answers

1. Mrs. McNab has heard the house will be sold and the family won't be back.

2. Mrs. McNab remembers Mrs. Ramsay as pleasant with all the staff. She envisions a specific day when Mrs. Ramsay, bent over her flowers, greets her warmly and tells her she will have the cook get her a plate of soup.

3. The house is near ruin. Something as weightless as a feather could tip the balance, making absolute disintegration inevitable.

4. The caretakers come to clean the house because they have received word from one of the Ramsay daughters that they will come to spend the summer and they want the house put into shape.

5. Mrs. McNab remembers Mr. Ramsay as an old gentleman, lean as a rake, wagging his head and talking to himself. He never spoke to her.

6. Mrs. McNab remembers the dinner parties, the guests in formal attire; she remembers the happy tone of the staff, the laughter in the kitchen; she recalls the tasty food, given generously by the cook.

7. The two women are in their seventies. They are slow in movement. They tire easily. They are not agile.

8. The messages of peace are messages that the war has ended.

9. Instead of being threatening and ominous, Nature becomes beautiful and gentle.

10. Lily's sleep is accompanied by the gentle waves and the tender night. She sleeps soundly and well.

Suggested Essay Topics

1. Write an essay in which you discuss Virginia Woolf's portrayal
    of Mrs. McNab. How does the writer depict the housekeeper's
    appearance, manner, and thought processes? Why did Woolf
    create this character to serve the function of heroine in this
    Time Passes?

2. Discuss why the Lighthouse might look with calmness at the
    decay. What does the Lighthouse signify in this section of
    the book? What might the Lighthouse symbolize?

The Lighthouse

Chapters I–II

New Character:

Mrs. Beckworth: *houseguest, kind, older woman; sketches*

Summary

"What does it mean then, what can it all mean?" Lily Briscoe asks herself the following morning. (See close of *Time Passes*) As she wanders through the house, she feels a kind of numbness coming back after all these years "and Mrs. Ramsay dead." It is a beautiful day and an expedition to the Lighthouse has been planned. Cam and James are not ready; Nancy has forgotten to order the sandwiches. Mr. Ramsay, annoyed with the children, has banged a door and now marches up and down on the terrace in a rage. Lily feels the house is chaotic and unreal. Nancy's dazed and desperate question, "What does one send to the Lighthouse?" strikes a nerve. Other questions bang around in her head, "What does one send? What does one do? Why is one sitting here, after all?"

Mr. Ramsay stops his preoccupied pacing for a moment and looks at Lily in a penetrating way. She wants to escape and pretends to drink out of her empty coffee cup, feeling his neediness. She hears his mumbled words ("alone" and "perished") as symbolic. She wishes she could create a sentence out of all the words in her head this morning. If she could, maybe she could get to the truth of things. Lily thinks that the unreality is frightening, but also

exciting: What does one send to the Lighthouse? Perished, alone, she repeats.

Suddenly Lily remembers a revelation about a painting she had had at this very table ten years ago. She had looked at a leaf pattern on the tablecloth and thought that she should move a tree to the middle. She remembers that she had never finished the painting and decides to paint that picture now. Setting up her easel in the same spot she had painted from long ago, she sees the wall, the hedge, and the tree and recalls that the problem was with the relation between those masses. Lily realizes that she has worked on this problem all these years and now she has the solution; she knows what she wants to do.

Mr. Ramsay's presence distracts her. She feels oppressed by him and can't paint. The evening before he had embarrassed her and the other guests by saying, "You find us much changed." She had sensed the children's discomfort and rage and had felt that the house was full of unrelated passions. Mr. Ramsay had demanded that they were going to the Lighthouse at the stroke of seven-thirty in the morning. She had felt, not only his demands, but also his histrionics, his gift for gesture. He had looked like a king in exile. Sixteen-year-old James and 17-year-old Cam had seemed to her the victims of a tragedy, their spirits had been subdued.

Returning to her canvas, Lily knows that when Mr. Ramsay is nearby she can't see colors or lines. She worries that he'll be upon her presently with his excessive demands. Lily becomes increasingly agitated and angry. She decides that Mr. Ramsay only takes and that Mrs. Ramsay had had to constantly give. Lily wishes she hadn't come. She feels pressured to feel something she doesn't feel. He will not let her paint, she thinks, until she gives him what he wants: sympathy. She supposes she must imitate the glow which Mrs. Ramsay, and other women, emanate when masculine need is so exposed.

Mr. Ramsay notices that Lily seems to have shriveled. He decides that she does not look unattractive. He is overcome with an enormous need to get sympathy from her. When he asks her if she has everything that she needs, Lily decides she can't do it; she can't fill his overwhelming need for sympathy. Bitterly, she decides she's a peevish, ill-tempered old maid. Mr. Ramsay continues to sigh and groan; she feels his dramatizing is indecent. He tells her that the journey to the Lighthouse will be painful. She feels she can't sustain the enormous weight of his grief. She decides that Ramsay's very looks seem to discolor the sunny grass, and place a funeral crepe over Mr. Carmichael, sitting reading nearby.

She, being a woman, has provoked this horror, Lily feels. She tells herself that it is immensely to her discredit, sexually, to stand there, dumb. His self pity, pouring in pools around her feet, only makes her want to draw her skirts closer, so that she doesn't get wet.

Lily hears Cam and James and begins to feel she may escape. When Ramsay notices his shoes are untied, Lily exclaims, "What beautiful boots!" She expects him to reject her for responding to his boots and not his emotional need, but he smiles and dives into a monologue about boots and bootmakers. He asks if she can tie a knot, then ties and unties her shoes three times to show her the correct way. As he stoops over her shoes, Lily is overcome with sympathy for him; tears well-up in her eyes. She thinks there is no helping him on the journey he is on, but now feels moved to speak to him. However, it is too late: James and Cam arrive, looking melancholy.

Ramsay's demeanor changes. As he takes charge of the parcels, he becomes like the leader of an expedition. The children's submission suggests to her that they have suffered beyond their years. Still, together, they look like a little company, moving off together.

Lily feels the sympathy she could not feel before. She reflects upon Mr. Ramsay's extraordinary face. She decides that thinking, night after night, about the reality of kitchen tables (remembering Andrew's image) has taken its toll. Mr. Ramsay has taken on the appearance of the unadorned table, an unornamented kind of beauty, which Lily admires. She decides that he must have had his doubts, about that table ("whether it was real, whether it was worth the time he gave to it, whether he was able, after all, to find it"). His need for others approval must be because of these doubts, Lily conjectures. She imagines that he must have shared his doubts with Mrs. Ramsay and that must have been exhausting for her.

As Lily watches the group disappear in the distance, she becomes aware of a different phase of Mr. Ramsay's emotions: he can suddenly become revitalized by something concrete (like the discussion about the boots); he can shed his worries, and recover his interest in ordinary things, entering another region; marching, as he did now, at the head of the little procession.

Analysis

The morning begins with Lily's question, "What does it mean then, what can it all mean? Lily's search for meaning provides the underpinning for the whole of *The Lighthouse*. Returning after all these years, Lily experiences a feeling of blankness. What, after all, has been the meaning of these lives?

Through Lily's eyes we see the current dysfunction of the family: Mr. Ramsay's helplessness, the children's anger and depression, and the disconnection they feel to each other ("a house full of unrelated passions"). She feels unnerved by what she senses as the symbolism of the words jumbling about in her head. Nancy's confusion about what to send to the Lighthouse stirs her.

Woolf uses Lily's stream-of-consciousness to suggest larger questions: "What does one take on one's journey through life? What is one to do on this journey? Why are we here, after all?" The journey is an important literary device which has rich metaphoric value. It is often used to suggest the human journey through life, the overcoming of obstacles, the movement toward a goal, the search for meaning.

Lily's struggle to somehow put together all these words and thoughts leads her to remember the unfinished painting. She becomes focused once again. She remembers the question was of the relation between the masses of the wall, the hedge, and the tree. Her search for correct relationships in her painting corresponds to her search (and Woolf's search) for understanding of the relationships she has so closely observed. Also, her earlier feeling of blankness and disorientation at the beginning of the day may be compared to that of the (artist) child trying to put together the family puzzle. Later in the day, the mature (artist) adult can place things in their proper relationships.

Mr. Ramsay is seen here as a helpless child. He has lost his anchor and he thrashes about for any female to comfort him. Woolf lays bare stereotyped gender expectations: Ramsay wants all women to mother him; Lily feels guilty about her "unwomanly" reaction, but resists his demands. In his presence she cannot see "color or line." Woolf's exploration of the needs of the artist, later developed more fully in the now-classic essay *A Room of One's Own*, reveals her own frustrations in accommodating womanly duties within the intellectual life.

Woolf discredits Lily's self-criticism by letting us see that she does respond deeply and sympathetically—when she is not being manipulated through role expectations. She is touched by Mr. Ramsay's childlike enthusiam over his boots and in tying her shoes. It is then that she feels his genuine vulnerability and neediness. She is moved to tears. When Mr. Ramsay regains his sense of self, organizing the expedition, Lily, relieved of a gender expectation, gains the distance she needs (as an artist) to admire him. She appreciates the rigor of his intellectual focus and senses that he (like she) is re-vitalized by the concrete world (the boots, the parcels, the expedition).

Study Questions

1. Why does Lily feel "blank" on the morning after she returns to the Ramsay house?

2. What is the mood in the household?

3. Why does Lily pretend to drink out of an empty coffee cup?

4. What words does Mr. Ramsay mutter to himself?

5. What does Lily remember about her unfinished painting?

6. What had Mr. Ramsay said to embarrass Lily and the other guests the evening before?

7. What are the children's feelings about going to the Lighthouse?

8. How does Lily feel about her behavior toward Mr. Ramsay?

9. How does Mr. Ramsay react to Lily's comment about his boots?

10. How do Lily's feelings about Mr. Ramsay change?

Answers

1. She wonders why she came back, now that Mrs. Ramsay is dead. She senses the conflict and disharmony in the house.

2. The mood is aimless, unreal, and chaotic. Doors slam and voices call all over the house.

3. Lily pretends to drink out of an empty cup, because she wants to avoid Mr. Ramsay's calls for sympathy.

4. Mr. Ramsay mutters "perished" and "alone" to himself.

5. Lily remembers that she had had a revelation ten years earlier at this very table. She had moved something on the tablecloth and had seen how she would fix up the composition of her painting.

6. Mr. Ramsay had said, "You find us much changed."

7. The children feel coerced. They agree to go to the Lighthouse, but they are not enthusiastic about the trip.

8. Lily feels she is a discredit to her gender. She knows she should be sympathetic, but she cannot be.

9. Mr. Ramsay is delighted with Lily's comment. He becomes absorbed in a discussion of boots and bootmakers.

10. Lily feels sympathy for Mr. Ramsay. She recognizes that he is bereft and has only the small escape of discussions about boots to comfort him. She admires his dedication to the quest for knowledge and his ability to put aside his worries and ambitions when he assumes command of his small expedition to the Lighthouse.

Suggested Essay Topics

1. Write an essay in which you discuss why Lily's sensibility as an artist is the vehicle Woolf uses to bring closure to the novel. Discuss how Lily's search for a solution to her painting problem mirrors her search for understanding and meaning.

2. What is Woolf saying here about male and female roles? How does Lily react to Mr. Ramsay's appeals for sympathy? How does she judge herself?

Chapter III

Summary

Lily returns to her painting. The white canvas rebukes her. She has been caught up in thoughts and feelings which have drained her emotions. As she ponders the problem of the relationship of the lines in the painting, she realizes that this challenge has tied a knot in her mind which over the years, at odd moments, she's tried to untangle.

In her agitation she's taken the wrong brush and placed the easel at the wrong angle. She corrects herself and sets about her work. Letting go of her emotional turmoil, she feels the excitement of the task. She paints the first stroke and then develops a rhythm in which she paints rapidly. As she works, Lily meditates on her reason for painting. She feels that to paint is to be engaged in a kind of combat. She begins to lose consciousness of the outer world, so concentrated is her effort.

While she works, the phrase, "can't paint, can't write" runs through her head. She remembers that Charles Tansley had said that about women. Then she recalls a windy morning when she and Tansley and Mrs. Ramsay were on the beach. As they noticed something in the water, Mrs. Ramsay had asked, "What is that? Is it a lobster-pot? An up-turned boat?" Suddenly, Charles' prickliness had fallen away and he had begun playing ducks and drakes with Lily. Mrs. Ramsay, sitting on a rock writing letters, seems to have been the catalyst to dispel the ill-will between her and Charles. It occurs to her that the memory of that day, so perfectly preserved, affects her like a work of art. She repeats this idea. It was Mrs. Ramsay's presence that was needed.

Then Lily asks herself, once again, "What is the meaning of life?" Mrs. Ramsay had made something permanent out of the fleeting moment. She was able to bring order out of chaos, ordering Life to stand still. Lily sees that as an artist that is what she tries to do. Perhaps this is the revelation she seeks, that one can find a shape under all the chaos.

Lily cries out, "Mrs. Ramsay! Mrs. Ramsay!" She feels she owes it all to her. Then, when she looks off in the distance, she sees a little boat shoot past the others, out to sea.

Analysis

Lily, the artist, like Virginia Woolf herself, needs to be alone to work. She is relieved when the Ramsay's boat sets off. Her canvas, the "problem" she seeks to solve, of line and relationship, has a magnetic pull. She can't allow herself to be distracted by the surface movement of daily life. She becomes absorbed in the rhythm of the painting and sees the work as a kind of combat.

Tansley's criticism of women, "Can't paint, can't write," runs through her mind. Thinking of Tansley, she remembers one special day on the beach with Mrs. Ramsay and the unhappy young man. The scene is etched in her mind and she realizes that it was Mrs. Ramsay's presence which shaped the scene and allowed it to be indelibly printed in her memory. It is Lily's gift as an artist (as it is Woolf's as a writer) to see the art of Mrs. Ramsay. Mrs. Ramsay was an artist of the heart, her presence created meaning for all who came near her.

This train of associations, begun with Lily's recall of Tansley's chauvinistic criticism, ends up with her awareness of Mrs. Ramsay's "feminine" gift, her ability to give meaning and shape to ordinary existence. Lily believes this is the revelation she's been seeking: there is shape under all the chaos. And, she now sees that in some curious way, Mrs. Ramsay has provided this for her.

Seeing a little boat—probably the Ramsays'—shooting out to sea, we connect Lily's important insight to the journey to the Lighthouse. Her intellectual journey occurs at the same time that the Ramsays move closer to their destination.

Study Questions

1. How does Lily feel as she returns to her painting?
2. As she paints, how do Lily's feelings change?
3. What is the image Lily has about painting?
4. What phrase recurs in Lily's mind?
5. What scene does Lily recall?
6. What was Mrs. Ramsay's part in that scene?
7. What revelation does Lily have about the meaning of life?

8. Why does Lily say she owes it all to Mrs. Ramsay?

9. What does Lily cry out?

10. What does Lily see when she looks out in the distance?

Answers

1. Lily feels rebuked by the canvas. She feels that her thoughts and feelings have drained her.

2. Lily becomes excited by the task and lets go of her emotional turmoil.

3. Lily thinks of painting like a kind of combat as she attacks her work.

4. Lily remembers that Tansley used to say that women "can't paint and can't write."

5. Lily remembers a windy morning at the beach when she and Tansley had played ducks and drakes.

6. Mrs. Ramsay's presence (asking about an object floating in the water, looking for her spectacles, etc.) had "oiled" the interaction between Lily and Charles. She had drained the tension from the two of them and had turned negative emotions into a harmonious encounter.

7. Lily sees that Mrs. Ramsay seemed to say, "Life stand still here!"; she had brought order out of chaos, as Lily seeks to do in her painting.

8. Lily feels Mrs. Ramsay's ability to create meaningful moments has shown Lily that finding shape under all the chaos is possible.

9. She cries out "Mrs. Ramsay, Mrs. Ramsay."

10. Lily sees a little boat shoot past the others, out to sea.

Suggested Essay Topics

1. The scene on the beach is an important one for Lily. Explain why this scene is important in terms of Lily's growing artistic sensibility.

2. Despite her strong intellectual convictions, Woolf thought about the supposed intellectual differences of men and women. Assuming that to some extent Lily personifies Woolf—and all female artists—explain what Woolf is saying about the encumbrances of gender on the artist.

Chapter IV

New Character:

Mr. Macalister: *seventy-five-year old fisherman; converses with Mr. Ramsay on the boat*

Summary

Out at sea, the boat is motionless. Mr. Ramsay, sitting in the middle, becomes impatient. He tells Macalister's boy to row.

James and Cam dread their father's impatience. They are angry that they have been bullied into the trip. They have sworn (silently) to "oppose tyranny to the death" and passively resist their father's commands. They hope there will be no breeze; they want their father's plans to be thwarted.

Suddenly, the boat takes off. Ramsay and Macalister share a pouch of tobacco and talk about a severe storm from the preceding winter. Three boats had sunk. The children sense their father likes this kind of man-against-nature story, where the men are heroic and the women sit around the fire with the children.

Cam thinks that her father would have been a brave leader of such a group. Hypnotized by the motion of the sea, the "pact" becomes loosened. James, too, becomes caught up now in fantasies of he and Cam escaping.

Mr. Ramsay points out their house on the distant shore. It's unreal to Cam; it's too far away. Her father imagines himself there, pacing up and down. He sees himself as old and desolate. Cam looks toward the island vaguely; she feels that it's in the past.

Mr. Ramsay teases her: Does she know the points of a compass? Cam, lost in thought, feels confused. Mr. Ramsay remembers his wife and thinks that all women are vague. Still, it's part of

their charm, he muses. He notices that she looks frightened and searches for something to talk to her about. Cam feels torn between her love for her father and her loyalty to her brother. James worries tensely that Cam will break down; she will not keep the pact. He has a dim memory of another scene, "They look down at their knitting or something. Then suddenly they look up." He thinks it must have been his mother and remembers he was very angry because she had "surrendered."

Cam thinks that her brother cannot know what a division of feeling she experiences. She adores her father—no one attracts her more—but she has suffered deeply from his "crass blindness and tyranny." She doesn't respond; she looks sadly at the shore and thinks that they have no suffering there.

Analysis

The atmosphere in the small boat is charged with intensity. James' rage escalates. As he watches his father and sister, the family drama is re-enacted. Will Cam, being female, give in to his tyrant father as his mother had? He has a vivid memory of the day his mother predicted he wouldn't forget.

Cam's suffering is palpable. Her conflicted feelings about her father, result in a kind of paralysis and her pre-occupation isolates her. She adores her father, romanticizes him, but cannot condone his autocratic behavior. She loses herself gazing at the water. When her father points out their house, she can only think that all those paths, "thick and knotted with the lives they had lived there, were gone; were rubbed out; were past; were unreal." Woolf's evocative rendering of Cam's depression, reminds the reader of Woolf's own mental illness.

As the children seethe internally, Mr. Ramsay appears unaware of the agony of feeling he evokes in them. Totally self-absorbed, he reads with his legs tightly curled. This small physical detail, repeated a number of times, suggests his lack of expansiveness in general. Virginia Woolf, like Lily Briscoe, prefers to suggest rather than spell out. Unlike writers who provide comprehensive descriptions of characters or settings, Woolf chooses to select a telling detail—the tightly curled legs—and repeat it so that the reader becomes aware that this particular posture has some special significance.

When the breeze picks up and the boat sails forward, Mr. Ramsay then uncurls his legs and opens his pouch of tobacco. He enjoys talking to the fisherman. The drama and romance of last winter's storm engage him. The children think that he likes the idea of men facing danger and women safely protected at home. Invigorated by the brisk sail, he cries out, "We perished, each alone." His spirits dampen as he sees the house in the distance and thinks of himself there. He imagines decrepitude, exhaustion and sorrow and his body begins to mirror his mental image. He repeats a line of poetry, "But I beneath a rougher sea/Was whelmed in deeper gulfs than he."

It is the (almost) unselfconscious way that Mr. Ramsay indulges his emotions that enrages the children. When he is comfortable, everyone else must be. When he is forlorn, others must run to his aid. His self-centeredness infuriates them; yet, his spontaneity and enthusiasm often seduce them.

Study Questions

1. What makes James and Cam nervous as they sit in the boat?

2. Why are James and Cam angry?

3. What is the topic of conversation between Mr. Ramsay and Macalister?

4. Why don't James and Cam take part in the conversation?

5. What is the pact that James and Cam share?

6. Why does James think Cam will "surrender"?

7. What does Mr. Ramsay think about as he looks back at the shore and their house?

8. What does Mr. Ramsay ask Cam about? What is his reaction to her confusion?

9. What are Cam's feelings toward her father?

10. What does Cam think about as she looks out to sea?

Answers

1. Cam and James know that their father does not like to wait; they dread his agitation and impatience.

2. James and Cam are angry because they feel they have been coerced to come on the trip.

3. Mr. Ramsay and Macalister talk about last winter's storm and a shipwreck.

4. James and Cam have made a vow to remain silent, to passively resist their father's tyranny.

5. James and Cam will resist tyranny to the death.

6. James remembers how his mother would surrender to his father, and he believes that all females will do that.

7. Mr. Ramsay sees himself as he was at the house, walking back and forth, between the urns. He sees himself as old, widowed, and desolate.

8. Mr. Ramsay first asks Cam about her puppy; he then asks her if she knows the points of the compass as she doesn't seem to be able to see the house. He is annoyed, because he feels all women are hopeless about such simple matters.

9. Cam has conflicting feelings about her father. She adores him, but she also detests his bullying.

10. Cam feels that the house in the distance is unreal— it is the past. She also feels that it is peaceful there.

Suggested Essay Topics

1. Discuss how the progress (or lack of progress) of the boat affects the passengers. What might be the symbolic value of being passengers in a sailboat? What happens to each person's mood when a sudden breeze propels the boat forward?

2. What are Cam's and Mr. Ramsay's thoughts as they look back at the island? What does the island represent to them now?

Chapters V–VII

New Character:

Macalister's son: *son of the fisherman who accompanies the Ramsays' on the boat*

Summary

Lily stands on the edge of the lawn, watching the Ramsay's boat sail off. She feels depressed about withholding her sympathy. She remembers Minta Doyle's flirtation with him and how it would lighten his mood. She almost asks Augustus Carmichael, sleeping in a lawn chair nearby, if he can remember these things.

Her thoughts return to Mrs. Ramsay and the day on the beach with Charles Tansley and herself. She wonders why that particular day, in all its detail, is so etched in her mind. Mrs. Ramsay's words, as she looked at something out at sea, echo in her head, "Is it a boat? Is it a cork?"

When Lily returns to her work, she muses that her painting must be beautiful and evanescent on the surface, but solid as iron underneath. She feels as if she is sitting beside Mrs. Ramsay on the beach. She remembers Mrs. Ramsay's preference for silence. She feels as if a door has opened, and she paints steadily.

Continuing to paint, her mind wanders back to the day on the beach with Mrs. Ramsay. Lily remembers noticing the hole in Minta Doyle's stocking. William Bankes had seemed to respond to her disorderliness with revulsion. She thinks of Minta's and Paul's marriage.

The marriage had not worked out. She creates a scene on a stairway, late at night where there is a disagreement. Creating such scenes is what we do, she thinks, and then we think we "know" people. In reality, Paul had told her that he "played chess in coffeehouses." This had led her to imagine an altercation late at night. Once when she visited them at their cottage she had felt the strain between them. Yet they seem to have gotten through this stage. They are now accepting of their alienation, and Paul has taken a mistress.

Lily imagines telling Mrs. Ramsay the story of the Rayleys, and she feels a bit smug. Continuing to paint, she decides that the dead

are at our mercy. Now that she is dead, we can brush aside all of
Mrs. Ramsay's old-fashioned ideas. Lily imagines her at the "end
of the corridor of years" saying, "Marry! Marry!" Lily feels for a
moment as if she's triumphed over Mrs. Ramsay; all had gone
against her wishes. The Rayley's marriage was not successful and
she, unmarried, was completely happy.

Lily asks herself why Mrs. Ramsay was so obsessed about marriage. Stirred by her thoughts about Paul Rayley, her mind conjures
up a dream-like scene, of savages dancing round a fire on a beach.
The phrase "in love" brings up powerful emotions that are com-
pelling, yet repulsive to her. She thinks that she had only escaped
by the skin of her teeth. She concludes that it was that moment at
dinner, ten years earlier, that she had suddenly seen the solution
to a painting, that she had felt triumphant, and that she really didn't
have to marry. Lily thinks about Mrs. Ramsay's authority and how
powerful she was.

Lily's memory of Mrs. Ramsay, sitting at the drawing room
window with James, leads her to think of William Bankes' queries
about her painting. His disinterested intelligence has comforted
and pleased her. His friendship is one of the pleasures of her life.
She admits that she loves William Bankes. They often stroll through
Hampton Court together, enjoying the stimulation of conversation
and art. One day he had spoken of his memory of Mrs. Ramsay, at
nineteen or twenty, looking astonishingly beautiful.

Returning her gaze to the drawing room steps, she imagines
Mrs. Ramsay with downcast eyes, sitting silently. She thinks that
beauty somehow covers over the more interesting, the more memo-
rable. What was the expression she would have worn at the odd
moment? Lily feels like asking Mr. Carmichael something, but she's
not sure what. The difficulty of communicating one's thoughts
overwhelms her. As she looks at the empty steps, a feeling of longing for whatever isn't there overwhelms her. She calls out silently
to Mrs. Ramsay.

Lily wants to ask Mr. Carmichael, "What does it mean? How
do you explain it?" She thinks that perhaps Carmichael, the inscru-
table poet, hears what she can't say. She begins to cry. She is
tormented by questions, "Was there no safety?" As tears roll down
her cheeks, she says aloud, "Mrs. Ramsay! Mrs. Ramsay!" An inter-

jection reports that Macalister's boy has cut a square out of one of the fish in the boat and baited his hook. He threw the mutilated body back to sea. Lily repeats her cry for Mrs. Ramsay. She is grateful that no one has heard her anguish. Slowly, she feels a sense of relief. She has a sense of Mrs. Ramsay by her side, but this ghost is relieved of the burdens she had carried. Lily again attacks the problem of painting the hedge. She envisions Mrs. Ramsay holding a wreath of white flowers to her forehead. She has imagined this scene many times since she heard of her death. She looked at the bay again and notices a brown spot. It is Mr. Ramsay's boat, halfway across the bay. She thinks of him in a vague sort of way. The morning is particularly fine, the sea and the sky look like one fabric. Lily thinks to herself, "Where are they now?"

Analysis

Although momentarily disturbed that she hadn't comforted Mr. Ramsay, Lily's focus and confidence are restored. Her thoughts alternate between the painting challenge before her and her reflections on Mrs. Ramsay. These thoughts are woven together in a complementary way. As she probes more deeply into Mrs. Ramsay's talent for creating meaning in human relationships, she gets closer to solving her painting problems.

Mrs. Ramsay is the catalyst that unleashes Lily's talent. Her inner dialogue becomes more concentrated as it shutttles back and forth between technical aesthetic problems and the meaning of Mrs. Ramsay's presence. Lily's thought about painting, "It should be beautiful and evanescent on the surface, but solid as iron underneath," seems to be almost a definition of Mrs. Ramsay.

In creating Lily and Mrs. Ramsay, Virginia Woolf explores her own aesthetic convictions. Lily's determination to disregard realistic details and to capture the essence of Mrs. Ramsay and her son parallels Woolf's literary ambitions. Lily's artistic image, developing art which is beautiful and evanescent on the surface, yet solid as iron underneath, emerges in the midst of her deep musing about Mrs. Ramsay, who personifies her objective. Mrs. Ramsay is a personification of Woolf's technique.

Woolf's uncanny ability to trace Lily's thoughts from the hole in Minta's stocking to the disappointment of the Rayley marriage

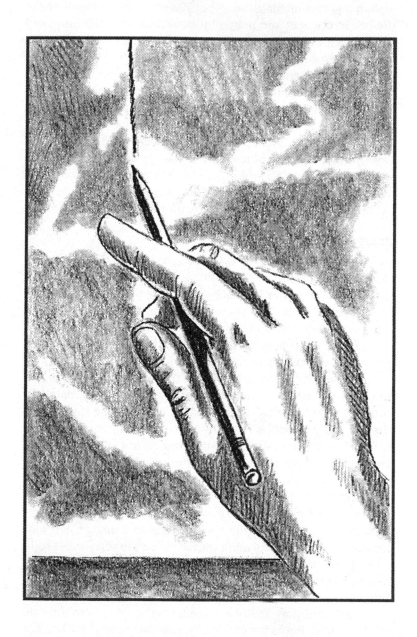

is yet another example of her expertise in the development of the stream-of-consciousness technique. She is able to hone in on the one detail that triggers a stream of thought which includes Lily's fantasies about the Rayley marriage, to her visits to them over the years, to Mrs. Ramsay's obsession about marriage, to her own marriageless odyssey. Woolf's execution of Lily's thoughts is a genuine tour-de-force.

Lily's relationship with William Bankes has proved to be far more satisfactory than Minta's and Paul's marriage. They enjoy a noncompetitive, mutually sustaining friendship which she regards as one of the pleasures of her life. Lily states simply that she loves William Bankes. Woolf's representation here of an equal partnership, suggests the kind of relationship she enjoyed with her husband, Leonard Woolf. Lily's consciousness of Bankes' infallible courtesy, offers up to the reader Woolf's recipe for a successful male-female bond, a more formal arrangement, in which social boundaries permit the relationship to flourish.

As she looks again at the drawing room steps, imagining Mrs. Ramsay there, she is overcome with the difficulty of communicating her thoughts. The empty steps become highly suggestive: they represent what isn't there, what can't be communicated: the mystery of life. Overcome, she sobs and calls out to Mrs. Ramsay. One may assume that the tears are not simply for the person of Mrs. Ramsay, but more the tears of a soul overcome by profound questions about the universe. As in life, Mrs. Ramsay continues to be the catalyst to allow Lily to explore the important questions.

The tears bring relief, and Lily feels that Mrs. Ramsay, relieved now of her burdens, is by her side. As she attacks "the problem of the hedge," she sees Mrs. Ramsay holding a wreath of flowers to her forehead. It should be noted that Woolf had imagined her beloved sister Stella, who died due to complications of a pregnancy, in much the same way.

The boat has become a mere speck in the water and her preoccupation with Mr. Ramsay has subsided. Her question, "Where are they now?" becomes more significant than its surface meaning. It suggests the larger question. Where is the family emotionally and psychologically? How have the Ramsays fared in resolving the issues which beset them?

Study Questions

1. Why does Lily feel depressed watching the Ramsay's boat sail off?
2. What does Lily feel like asking Mr. Carmichael?
3. What memory is etched in Lily's mind?
4. What is Lily's goal for her painting?
5. How has the Rayley marriage turned out?
6. Describe Lily's relationship with William Bankes.
7. Why does Lily call out to Mrs. Ramsay?
8. Why does Lily cry?
9. How does Lily envision Mrs. Ramsay as she paints?
10. What does Lily ask as she looks out to sea?

Answers

1. Lily feels depressed that she hasn't given Mr. Ramsay the sympathy that he had wanted.
2. Lily feels like asking Carmichael if he remembers the Ramsays and Minta Doyle as she does.
3. Lily recalls vividly one particular day at the beach. Mrs. Ramsay had been writing letters, sitting on a rock. She had looked up and seeing something in the waves had searched for her spectacles. She had asked, "Is it a boat? Is it a cork?" Mrs. Ramsay somehow managed to lighten Charles Tansley's mood, and Lily and Charles had been more companionable than heretofore.
4. Lily wants her painting to be beautiful and evanescent on the surface, but solid as iron underneath.
5. The Rayley marriage has not turned out well. Paul spends a lot of time in coffeehouses. Lily has observed the tension and unhappiness of the couple.
6. Lily and William Bankes have enjoyed a mutually satisfying friendship. They enjoy discussing art and ideas. They spend pleasant days together.

7. Lily calls out to Mrs. Ramsay when she looks at the empty steps and feels a longing for what isn't there. The emptiness suggests to her the difficulty of communicating one's thoughts.

8. Lily cries because she is overcome with thoughts of the enigma of life: What does it mean? As thoughts about the uncertainty of life (Was there no safety?) overcome her, tears roll down her cheeks, and she calls out again to Mrs. Ramsay.

9. Lily envisions Mrs. Ramsay sitting by her side. She also sees her holding a wreath of white flowers to her forehead.

10. Lily asks, "Where are they now?" Her question encompasses more than the Ramsay's progress at sea. It suggests where they are emotionally.

Suggested Essay Topics

1. Lily wants her painting to be "beautiful and evanescent on the surface, but solid as iron underneath." Explain how this is a description of Virginia Woolf's goals as a novelist. How does she accomplish this in *To the Lighthouse*?

2. Write an essay about Lily's perceptions of marriage. Include her fantasy about savages dancing around a fire on the beach.

Chapters VIII–X

Summary

Cam trails her hand in the water and looks at the distant shore. She thinks that they don't feel anything there. The wind stops, the sails sag, the boat is calm. It seems as if the world is standing still. Under the hot sun, they feel miles from the shore, miles from the Lighthouse. Mr. Ramsay continues to read with his legs curled under him. James dreads the moment when his father will look up and demand why they aren't moving. Each page Mr. Ramsay turns feels like a hostile gesture aimed at him. James thinks that if his father makes an unreasonable demand, he will take a knife and strike him to the heart. Aware that he's held onto this old image, James decides that it's not exactly the old man sitting across from him that he wants to kill, but rather something that seems to descend on him, "a black-winged harpy with talons and a hard beak that has struck him repeatedly." He remembers the beak striking him when he was a child. He thinks that whatever he becomes in life—a banker, a barrister, a businessman—he will stamp out that kind of aggression ("tyranny, despotism"). Still, James knows that his father can be admirable, "pressing a sovereign into some old woman's hand." Lately, he has felt that he and his father are alike. He asks himself, "What then was this terror, this hatred?" The image he conjures up is of a wagon wheel, ignorantly and innocently, crushing someone's foot.

James remembers gardens, an old woman gossiping in the kitchen, and a dress rustling. It was in this happy world, that the wheel went over the person's foot. His father had said, "It will rain. You won't be able to go to the Lighthouse." He remembers the Lighthouse as a silver, misty tower with a yellow eye that opened suddenly in the evening. Now he sees that the Lighthouse is really a stark tower with black and white bars. James' strain is acute. As he imagines the rustle of someone coming, he worries that his father will suddenly slap his book down and demand to know why they are dawdling. He remembers that once before his father had brought his blade down on the terrace and his mother had gone stiff all over. She had gotten up and left him on the floor feeling impotent, as he grasped a pair of scissors. James wonders where his mother had gone that day. He pictures himself following her, hearing her speak naturally to a servant. James knows that that was what he most admired, that one could say anything to her. With his hands on the tiller, James stares at the Lighthouse and feels powerless. He feels bound by a rope his father has knotted. His only escape would be to take a knife and plunge it. Then the breeze picks up and the boat takes off. James is enormously relieved. Mr. Ramsay doesn't even look up, but lifts his right hand in the air as if he's conducting a symphony. (Lily Briscoe, looking out over the bay, feels that distance has swallowed the boat up. She feels as if the Ramsays are gone forever. Smoke from a steamer hangs in the air like a mournful flag.)

Drawing her fingers once again through the waves, Cam looks at the shape of the island from a distance. It looks like a leaf, standing on one end. She starts to imagine a shipwreck story, then decides that she doesn't want a story, but the sense of adventure and escape she's beginning to feel. As the boat takes off, her father's anger about the points of the compass and James' obstinacy about their compact, all stream away. She asks herself, "What comes next? Where are they going?" Holding her hand in the ice-cold water, she feels joy that she's alive.

Cam thinks of Mr. Carmichael, Mr. Bankes and her father in the study. She used to stray in from the garden to catch them in their talk, their reading and writing. She had felt safe there to think her thoughts. She had felt her father's kindness there. As Cam watches her father read, she returns to her internal dialogue with James. She imagines pointing out that he's not a tyrant, at least not now. She imagines her father guiding or wheedling a flock of sheep as he reads, pushing his way up a narrow path. She goes on telling herself a story about escaping from a sinking ship. She feels safe with him reading there, as she had felt in the library long ago. The island is very distant. She dabbles her fingers in the water and murmurs dreamily "how we perished, each alone."

Analysis

The becalming of the boat mirrors the paralysis James and Cam feel. They are stuck in the boat and stuck in their early emotions. The rage James felt as a child is very close to the surface here. He is in a state of perpetual anxiety, anticipating his father's impulsive and arbitrary behavior. His old "symbol," the fantasy of stabbing his father through the heart, is as vivid now as it was when he was six-years-old. Cam is tormented with divided loyalties and is preoccupied with melancholy thoughts, i.e., the people on the island don't have to feel. She daydreams and longs to escape.

James' inner life is communicated dramatically in this section. Mrs. Ramsay's prediction was prescient: that day is etched in his memory. Although in his maturity he understands that he doesn't really hate the man sitting across from him, he knows that in some moment, long ago, his feelings had crystallized around a frightening image associated with his father. James has imagined his father becoming a black-winged harpy with sharp talons striking his bare legs. We, of course, recall his father's trying to restore his good humor by switching him playfully on the legs (Mr. Ramsay's attempt to "make up" for the fact that they couldn't go to the Lighthouse). In addition to this dark memory, James recalls the image of a wagon wheel crushing a bare foot. Delving deeper into his memories, he knows there was a day that his father had brought something sharp down on the terrace (we remember his father expostulating, "Damn you!" to Mrs. Ramsay, objecting to her lack of "practicality"). He remembers his mother's body stiffening and then her getting up and leaving him. A flood of dim memories are associated with this: the rustling of a dress, whispers, lights, etc.

James' preoccupation with these disturbing images is suddenly interrupted when the breeze picks up and the boat shoots forward. Mr. Ramsay, totally unaware of the agony he is causing his son, lifts his hand like the conductor of a symphony. This gesture is reminiscent of other dramatic gestures we have seen. We sense that he is always listening to an innner orchestra and that his impatience is not so much directed at his children or others, but at his own need for harmony and order and progress.

The rapid movement of the boat stirs Cam also. She experiences a "fountain of joy" as her hand moves through the cold water. She has felt "deadened" almost the whole journey. Now, her sense of story, reasserts itself, "What comes next? Where are we going?" Cam's questions, like the other questions this day, suggest more than the immediate. The questions are really about Life, the Ramsays' life, and that of the larger world.

It is interesting to contrast the comfort and security Cam felt as a child in her father's study, with the frustration and rage her brother felt. The two have had different experiences and different needs. Cam's reveries haven't included her mother; she only has a melancholy feeling about all of that being far away. She seems to have derived real sustenance from her father. This is not unlike the bond Virginia Woolf felt for her father. In an early conversation with her sister Vanessa, Virginia asked who was the better parent. Virginia's answer was her father.

Study Questions

1. What happens to the boat out at sea?
2. What are Cam's thoughts about the distant island?
3. What are James' thoughts and feelings about his father?
4. What memories come to James' mind?
5. What does James want to do to his father?
6. What are Cam's thoughts about her father and brother?
7. How does the sudden progress of the boat affect James, Cam, and Mr. Ramsay?
8. How did Cam feel as a child when she had sat with her father and Carmichael and Bankes in the study?
9. What is Cam's image of her father reading?
10. What does Cam murmer dreamily to herself as she looks at the distant island?

Answers

1. The boat is becalmed. There is no breeze.
2. Cam feels that they don't feel anything there.
3. James feels that every gesture Mr. Ramsay makes is a hostile gesture directed at him. He anticipates with dread an unreasonable outburst from his father. He summons up the old image of stabbing his father in the heart.
4. James has a string of memories: he imagines his father as a black-winged harpy, striking his leg with its beak; he remembers the gardens, a dress rustling, and women gossiping. He remembers his father saying, "It will rain. You won't be able to go to the Lighthouse." He remembers a wagon wheel had gone over a person's foot.
5. James wants to stab his father in the heart.
6. Cam feels upset by her father's criticisms, i.e., she didn't know the points of the compass and pressured by James' obstinacy about their compact.

7. James feels relieved by the sudden movement of the boat. Mr. Ramsay lifts his hand as if he's conducting a symphony. Cam feels a sense of adventure and escape as well as a sudden joy and anticipation.

8. Cam had felt safe to think her own thoughts in the study. She had felt her father's kindness there.

9. Cam imagines her father guiding a flock of sheep up a narrow path, as he reads.

10. Cam repeats her father's words, "We perished, each alone."

Suggested Essay Topics

1. Write an essay in which you show that Mrs. Ramsay's worry that James would remember that day for the rest of his life was foresight.

2. Examine James' and Cam's different memories of their father. Write a "psychological evaluation" of the two adolescents. What role might gender play in their different experiences?

Chapters XI–XIII

Summary

Lily watches the boat sail off. She decides that so much depends upon distance, whether people are near or far away. Lily thinks again of the unreality of the morning and decides that life is more vivid when routine hasn't quite taken hold. She feels relieved of the burden of making pleasantries with Mrs. Beckworth. The interlude is full to the brim with so many interwoven lives held by some common feeling. It was this feeling that led her to say, a decade before, that she was in love with the place.

Looking out to sea, Lily notices a change in the wind and the placement of the boats. The disproportion disturbs her and she looks at her painting with distress. She's wasted her morning and has not been able to keep the requisite "razor's edge of balance" between her painting and Mr. Ramsay. Determined to recapture her vision, Lily realizes that the words and ideas in her head are getting in the way. She wants to get that "very jar on the nerves" which precedes the naming of something. Her urgency, too, gets in the way. How can she paint, if she can't think or feel?

Lily sits on the grass, thinking that everything today seemed to be happening for the first or the last time. She imagines that Augustus Carmichael, lounging nearby, is sharing her thoughts. He is now a famous poet and no more communicative than he's ever been. His poetry must be somewhat impersonal, she thinks. She had sensed that he didn't like Mrs. Ramsay.

Thinking about Mr. Carmichael and Mrs. Ramsay, she realizes that many people must have disliked Mrs. Ramsay. They may have found her too self-assured, or too beautiful. Lily realizes that Mrs. Ramsay's instinct was to minister to others, "turning her infallibly to the human race, making her nest in its heart." People like she and Mr. Carmichael, who preferred thought to action, were annoyed by Mrs. Ramsay's directness.

Lily is reminded of Charles Tansley (who also upset others). She had once heard him giving a lecture, preaching brotherly love. Although she still found him irritating, she had remembered the day on the beach when an old cask had bobbed in the waves and Mrs. Ramsay had searched for her spectacles. Tansley had been amused by Mrs. Ramsay's exaggerations and had smiled charmingly. Lily thinks that it was only through Mrs. Ramsay's eyes that she could look without abhorrence at Tansley.

Fifty pairs of eyes are needed to see Mrs. Ramsay, Lily decides. What did Mrs. Ramsay think of the garden, the hedge, the children? She remembers Mrs. Ramsay's embarrassment when Mr. Ramsay stopped near her. He had stretched his hand out and raised her from her chair. Had she said she would marry him once in this identical pose? Lily feels that despite the confusion of children and guests, there were repetitions, or vibrations that echoed in the air. Yet, their closeness was no "monotony of bliss." There were scenes, slamming of doors, plates hurled out of windows, and rigid silences. She would become remote and withdrawn. Mr. Ramsay would skulk about, trying to get her attention. After a time, he would call out to her and they would walk off together in the gardens. Later, at dinner, things would return to normal with laughing and joking.

Lily glances at the window and notices a triangular shadow on the steps caused by someone in the drawing room. Her painting mood returns. She wants to hold the scene in a vise, to become one with the objects before her. A stirring in the room moves her to call out to Mrs. Ramsay. Her old horror returns, then quickly subsides. It is as if Mrs. Ramsay has sat down with her knitting. She walks to the edge of the lawn and wonders where Mr. Ramsay is now.

On the boat, Mr. Ramsay has almost finished reading. He looks very old, James decides. As they near the Lighthouse, James sees that it is a stark tower on a bare rock. It satisfies him. He identifies with it and senses that his father does too. He says to himself, "We are driving before a gale—we must sink," much as his father would have said. None of them have spoken for a long time. James and Cam again vow silently that they will fight tyranny to the death. Cam feels that her father, lost in his book, always escapes. As she looks back at the tiny dot of the island, she thinks of the terraces, and bedrooms and paths that were there. As she looks drowsily at the island, she thinks it is a hanging garden full of birds and flowers.

Mr. Ramsay shuts his book and opens the lunch parcels. Macalister praises James' steering. His father says nothing. James sees that his father is happy eating bread and cheese with the fishermen. Cam feels safe in her father's presence. She is excited as the boat nears the rocks. Macalister says that they (he and Mr. Ramsay) will soon be out of it, but that their children will see some strange things. Cam feels her father is leading them on a great expedition.

Macalister points to the spot where three men have drowned. James and Cam dread another outburst. They are afraid their father will say, once again, "But I beneath a rougher sea." But all Mr. Ramsay says is "Ah." He lights his pipe, looks at his watch and then says triumphantly to James, "Well done!" for James had steered them "like a born sailor." Cam thinks, "There! You've got it at last!" Sailing up to the reef, they see two men getting ready to meet them. Cam and James watch their father looking intently back at the island. They wonder if he is thinking, "We perished each alone," or "I have reached it. I have found it." Mr. Ramsay puts on his hat and stands tall in the boat, ordering the parcels to be brought. He leaps, like a young man, onto the rock.

Back on the island, Lily thinks, "He must have reached it." She is exhausted with the effort of looking at the Lighthouse and thinking of him landing there, but she thinks that whatever he had wanted this morning, she had given him. She says out loud, "He has landed," and "It is finished." Carmichael, like an old pagan god, shaggy with weeds in his hair, gets up and says, "'They will have landed." Lily decides that they had, after all, been thinking the same thing. Carmichael's presence seems to crown the occasion.

Quickly, Lily returns to her picture. It will be hung in the attics, but that doesn't matter. She looks at the empty steps; she looks at the canvas. It is blurred. With a sudden intensity, "as if she saw it clear for a second," she draws a line in the center. "It was done; it was finished." She lays down her brush, in extreme fatigue, and thinks, "I have had my vision."

Analysis

In these last chapters, Woolf not only brings closure to the book, but illuminates her creative process. As we follow Lily's stream-of-consciousness, we glimpse the evolution of Woolf's own "vision." Woolf herself said that in the beginning, Lily was a minor character in her mind, but that as the writing progressed, the artist had formed the central consciousness of the book.

There is a rhythm in Lily's alternating focus—looking out to the sea, then back at her painting. Her attention moves from reflection and contemplation about the meaning of lives and relationships to the more abstract problem of creating aesthetic meaning. Tracing her associative process, Woolf accomplishes precisely what Lily herself seeks to achieve. Lily thinks,

> What was the problem then? She must try to get hold of something that evaded her. It evaded her when she thought of Mrs. Ramsay; it evaded her now when she thought of her picture. Phrases came. Visions came. Beautiful pictures. Beautiful phrases. But what she wished to get hold of was *that very jar on the nerves*, the thing itself before it has been made anything. Get that and start afresh; get that and start afresh; she

said desperately, pitching herself firmly again before her easel. It was a miserable machine, an inefficient machine, she
thought, the human apparatus for painting or for feeling; it
always broke down at the critical moment; heroically one
must force it on.

We glimpse Woolf's struggle to capture the evanescent moment,
to convey real experience and not a mere description of experience. Beautiful phrases alone don't create meaning. She (and Lily)
want to capture not a scene, but a feeling about a scene, the split-
second when the mind perceives meaning.

As Lily watches the Ramsay'ssboat sail into the distance, she
reflects that so much depends upon distance, whether people are
near or far away. What is suggested here is not physical distance
alone, but the distance of time. Time has been a continuous thread
throughout the novel. In *The Window*, the characters are absorbed
in speculation about the future: "Will we go to the Lighthouse tomorrow?", "Will James remember this all of his life?" "What future
lies in store for Prue? for Minta? for Lily?" "Will Mr. Ramsay make
R"? How will his work be appraised in the future?" "Will this candle-
lit dinner stay in our memory in the future?" *Time Passes* is entirely about the passage of time: How are human structures treated
by time and nature? How do events in the world impact on human
lives? How does time obliterate what has been? In *The Lighthouse*,
the characters are caught up in understanding the meaning of the
past and finding a direction for the future.

Again, Lily's meditation on distance ("whether people are near
or far away") echoes Woolf's own experience. Writing in *To the
Lighthouse* about her own parents, she has gained a more detached
objectivity. Lily now sees that her much-adored Mrs. Ramsay (mod-
eled on Julia Stephen) must have been disliked by many people.
Her physical beauty, as well as her social self-confidence, must have
intimidated or aggravated some.

Throughout *The Lighthouse*, Lily is disturbed by the "unreality" of the day—normal human activity seems suspended. Yet, it is
this "unreal" quality that jars her thinking and observation and
allows new insight and understanding. This is another kind of
distance, a state of mind unencumbered by social routine. The

distraction of social convention, in particular the obligation to make small talk, is a constant threat to Lily.

Lily's memory of Mrs. Ramsay searching for her spectacles leads to her thought that to see Mrs. Ramsay one needs 50 pairs of eyes. Once again, Woolf has triumphed in her brilliant use of the stream-of-consciousness. She has captured, probably as well as any writer, the true workings of the mind. Is it ever possible for the writer or artist to capture the whole of a person?

Lily perceives pattern and meaning ("vibrations") in the Ramsays domestic life. Looking beyond and beneath the surface confusion and tension, she sees the shape of the marriage. The reader feels that it is her ability to connect these random events that finally opens her mind to the correct proportions for her painting.

As Lily walks to the edge of the lawn, wondering where Mr. Ramsay is now, the two journeys—the Ramsays' and her own—are more deeply enmeshed. All of Lily's questions suggest more than superficial queries. Where is Mr. Ramsay now in terms of his needs, his sorrows, his personal journey?

Nearing the Lighthouse, James is able not only to see the Lighthouse for what it is—"a stark tower on a bare rock," but also to see his father more realistically, (he looks very old). His internal dialogue mirrors his father's, "We are driving before a gale—we must sink."

Cam's reverie about the island being a hanging garden full of birds and flowers echoes the story her mother told to soothe her in the nursery. Her memories are less specific than James'. Cam thinks with her heart and feelings about her parents.

Macalister's remark to Mr. Ramsay that they will be out of it soon, but the children will see some strange things, is a barely noticeable reference to the fallout of the first World War.

The culmination of the trip occurs when Mr. Ramsay compliments James on his sailing. James has been waiting for his father's approval for his whole life. They have not only finally made it to the Lighthouse, but the child's rage has been assuaged.

In the last scene, back on the island, Lily feels the exhaustion of looking at the Lighthouse and thinking of Ramsay landing there. Lily, the artist, not only has struggled with her picture, but with her identification with the emotional and psychological struggles of the family. Her words, "It is finished" may be an analogy of the words spoken by Jesus at his crucifixtion. In some mysterious way, her quest for proportion and harmony, as well as understanding, has enabled the others to experience peace.

Lily's sudden completion of her painting, through blurred eyes, culminates her wish to capture the very jar of the nerves and not a thought about a scene.

Study Questions

1. What is Lily's thought as the boat recedes in the distance?
2. How does Lily feel about routine? Social convention?
3. What does Lily want to capture in her painting?
4. What is Lily's intuition about Mr. Carmichael's poetry?
5. Why might people have disliked Mrs. Ramsay?
6. What positive memory does Lily have of Charles Tansley?
7. Was the Ramsay marriage blissful, according to Lily?
8. What is the conversation between Macalister and Mr. Ramsay?
9. What does Cam mean when she thinks, "There! You've got it at last?"
10. Why is Lily exhausted?

Answers

1. Lily thinks that so much depends upon distance.
2. Lily feels that when routine is broken, one can see life more clearly.
3. Lily wants to capture "the jar on the nerves" of human experience, not a description of it.
4. Lily thinks that his poetry must be impersonal.
5. Some people may have been intimidated by her beauty or her interventions.

6. Lily remembers a day at the beach when somehow Mrs. Ramsay's presence allowed Tansley to lighten up and be playful.

7. The Ramsays' marriage was not a "monotony of bliss" according to Lily. She remembers certain scenes, slammed doors, plates thrown out of windows, and rigid silences.

8. Macalister tells Ramsay about a shipwreck which happened the preceding winter. Three men had drowned.

9. Cam thinks that James has finally gotten his father's approval when his father says, "Well done!" commenting on James' sailing.

10. Lily is exhausted with the effort of following the Ramsays' boat and worrying about their journey. Her effort to complete her picture is tied in her mind to the Ramsays' reaching the Lighthouse.

Suggested Essay Topics

1. When Lily completes her picture, we sense that more than the painting is completed. What has been necessary for her to have her vision?

2. In an essay explain the meaning of the title of the book. What is the significance of the Lighthouse to the main characters?

Sample Analytical Paper Topics

These are topics on which you can write a substantial analytical paper. They are designed to test your understanding of major themes and details from this novel as a whole. Following topics are outlines you can use as a starting point for writing an analytical paper.

Topic #1

Woolf's development of the "stream of consciousness" technique in this novel is regarded by most critics as a *tour de force*. Identify several examples of this technique and discuss how a character's inner thoughts (words and images): (a) provide an in-depth understanding of his/her character; (b) illustrate the associative intelligence of the mind in the process of understanding and creative expression.

Outline

I. Thesis Statement: *Woolf uses the "stream of consciousness" technique to reveal characters in depth and to illustrate the associative intelligence of the mind.*

II. Mrs. Ramsay's "stream of consciousness"

III. Lily Briscoe's "stream of consciousness"

IV. Mr. Ramsay's "stream of consciousness"

V. James Ramsay's "stream of consciousness"

VI. The "stream of consciousness" technique as a means to reveal associative mental processes

Topic #2

Gender is an important theme in the novel. Give examples of role definitions or expectations for men and for women in *To the Lighthouse* and situations where sterotypical definitions or expectations are resisted or abandoned.

Outline

I.   Thesis Statement: *Woolf explores various aspects of gender definition and expectation, as well as providing counter-examples of sterotyped role expectations.*

II. Mrs. Ramsay as quintessential feminine personae

III. Mr. Ramsay as sterotyped Victorian male

IV. Lily Briscoe as artist who resists role expectations

V.   Cam as young modern woman, with divided loyalties

Topic #3

In *To the Lighthouse*, Woolf analyzes the creative process. The evolution of Lily Briscoe's emotional and creative abilities is the subtext of the novel. Analyze Briscoe's artistic development and explore its implications in terms of understanding the novel.

Outline

I.   Thesis Statement: *Woolf illuminates the creative process through Lily Briscoe's emotional, psychological, and artistic growth. Her growth is the subtext of the novel.*

II. Lily's artistic counsciousness during *The Window*

III. Lily's place in *Time Passes*

IV. Lily's artistic development in *The Lighthouse*

V.   Significant moments in Lily's artisic growth

SECTION SIX

Bibliography

Qutotations from *To the Lighthouse* are taken from the following edition:

Woolf, Virginia. *To the Lighthouse*. *Foreword* by Eudora Welty. New York: Harcourt Brace & Company, 1927.

The following works were often consulted during the course of this work:

Auerbach, Erich, "The Brown Stocking" in his *Mimesis: The Representation of Reality in Western Literature*, trans., Willard Trask (Princeton University Press, 1953).

Abel, Elizabeth, *Virginia Woolf and the Fictions of Psychoanalysis* (Chicago University Press, 1989).

Beja, Morris, *Virginia Woolf's To the Lighthouse: A Casebook* (Macmillan, 1970).

Bell, Quentin, *Virginia Woolf: A Biography*, 2 vols. (Hogarth Press, 1972).

Blotner, Joseph, *Mythic patterns in To the Lighthouse*, Proceedings of the Modern Language Association 71 (1956, pp. 547-62).

DiBattista, Maria, *Virginia Woolf's Major Novels: The Fables of Anon* (Yale University Press, 1980).

Gordon, Lyndall, *Virginia Woolf: A Literary Life* (Macmillan, 1991).

Leaska, Mitchell A., *The Novels of Virginia Woolf: From Beginning to End* (John Jay Press, 1977).

Lee, Hermone, "To the Lighthouse" in *Virginia Woolf: Introduction to the Major Works*, ed. Julia Briggs (Virago Press, 1994).

Richter, Harvena, *Virginia Woolf: The Inward Voyage* (Princeton University Press, 1970).

Ruotolo, Lucio P., *The Interrupted Moment: A View of Virginia Woolf's Novels* (Stanford University Press, 1986).

MAXnotes®

REA's Literature Study Guides

MAXnotes® are student-friendly. They offer a fresh look at masterpieces of literature, presented in a lively and interesting fashion. **MAXnotes®** offer the essentials of what you should know about the work, including outlines, explanations and discussions of the plot, character lists, analyses, and historical context. **MAXnotes®** are designed to help you think independently about literary works by raising various issues and thought-provoking ideas and questions. Written by literary experts who currently teach the subject, **MAXnotes®** enhance your understanding and enjoyment of the work.

Available **MAXnotes®** include the following:

Absalom, Absalom!
The Aeneid of Virgil
Animal Farm
Antony and Cleopatra
As I Lay Dying
As You Like It
The Autobiography of
    Malcolm X
The Awakening
Beloved
Beowulf
Billy Budd
The Bluest Eye, A Novel
Brave New World
The Canterbury Tales
The Catcher in the Rye
The Color Purple
The Crucible
Death in Venice
Death of a Salesman
The Divine Comedy I: Inferno
Dubliners
Emma
Euripides' Medea & Electra
Frankenstein
Gone with the Wind
The Grapes of Wrath
Great Expectations
The Great Gatsby
Gulliver's Travels
Hamlet
Hard Times

Heart of Darkness
Henry IV, Part I
Henry V
The House on Mango Street
Huckleberry Finn
I Know Why the Caged
    Bird Sings
The Iliad
Invisible Man
Jane Eyre
Jazz
The Joy Luck Club
Jude the Obscure
Julius Caesar
King Lear
Les Misérables
Lord of the Flies
Macbeth
The Merchant of Venice
The Metamorphoses of Ovid
The Metamorphosis
Middlemarch
A Midsummer Night's Dream
Moby-Dick
Moll Flanders
Mrs. Dalloway
Much Ado About Nothing
My Antonia
Native Son
1984
The Odyssey
Oedipus Trilogy

Of Mice and Men
On the Road
Othello
Paradise Lost
A Passage to India
Plato's Republic
Portrait of a Lady
A Portrait of the Artist
    as a Young Man
Pride and Prejudice
A Raisin in the Sun
Richard II
Romeo and Juliet
The Scarlet Letter
Sir Gawain and the
    Green Knight
Slaughterhouse-Five
Song of Solomon
The Sound and the Fury
The Stranger
The Sun Also Rises
A Tale of Two Cities
The Taming of the Shrew
The Tempest
Tess of the D'Urbervilles
Their Eyes Were Watching God
To Kill a Mockingbird
To the Lighthouse
Twelfth Night
Uncle Tom's Cabin
Waiting for Godot
Wuthering Heights

REA's Test Preps
The Best in Test Preparation

- REA "Test Preps" are far **more** comprehensive than any other test preparation series
- Each book contains up to **eight** full-length practice exams based on the most recent exams
- **Every** type of question likely to be given on the exams is included
- Answers are accompanied by **full** and **detailed** explanations

REA has published over 60 Test Preparation volumes in several series. They include:

Advanced Placement Exams (APs)
Biology
Calculus AB & Calculus BC
Chemistry
Computer Science
English Language & Composition
English Literature & Composition
European History
Government & Politics
Physics
Psychology
Spanish Language
United States History

College Level Examination Program (CLEP)
American History I
Analysis & Interpretation of Literature
College Algebra
Freshman College Composition
General Examinations
Human Growth and Development
Introductory Sociology
Principles of Marketing

SAT II: Subject Tests
American History
Biology
Chemistry
French
German
Literature

SAT II: Subject Tests (continued)
Mathematics Level IC, IIC
Physics
Spanish
Writing

Graduate Record Exams (GREs)
Biology
Chemistry
Computer Science
Economics
Engineering
General
History
Literature in English
Mathematics
Physics
Political Science
Psychology
Sociology

ACT - American College Testing Assessment

ASVAB - Armed Service Vocational Aptitude Battery

CBEST - California Basic Educational Skills Test

CDL - Commercial Driver's License Exam

CLAST - College Level Academic Skills Test

ELM - Entry Level Mathematics

ExCET - Exam for Certification of Educators in Texas

FE (EIT) - Fundamentals of Engineering Exam

FE Review - Fundamentals of Engineering Review

GED - High School Equivalency Diploma Exam (US & Canadian editions)

GMAT - Graduate Management Admission Test

LSAT - Law School Admission Test

MAT - Miller Analogies Test

MCAT - Medical College Admission Test

MSAT - Multiple Subjects Assessment for Teachers

NTE - National Teachers Exam

PPST - Pre-Professional Skills Tests

PSAT - Preliminary Scholastic Assessment Test

SAT I - Reasoning Test

SAT I - Quick Study & Review

TASP - Texas Academic Skills Program

TOEFL - Test of English as a Foreign Language

RESEARCH & EDUCATION ASSOCIATION
61 Ethel Road W. • Piscataway, New Jersey 08854
Phone: (908) 819-8880

Please send me more information about your Test Prep Books

Name _____

Address _____

City _____ State _____ Zip _____